MW00994629

Abusive Power:

When Christians Hurt

Other Christians

The Living Well Series, Volume 8

The Living Well Series

(See http://www.pastorselfcare.com)

Volume 1: *Finishing Well: Retirement Skills for Ministers.*
Available at www.createspace.com/3789682. Ministers face much more difficult retirement issues than most secular individuals. They not only lose their occupation, but they often lose friends, identity, self-esteem and too frequently, even their future hope of effective ministry. This book provides ministers with skills to know when it is time to retire, how to gracefully transition to a new ministry, and how to survive and thrive like never before.

Volume 2: *Transforming Conflict: Relationship Skills for Ministers.*
Available at www.createspace.com/3856947. This book helps ministers prevent church discord even while enhancing relationships. This book helps individuals learn:
- How to prevent and eliminate relationship obstacles
- How to cultivate research-proven relationship skills
- How to adapt each relationship skill to their ministry

Volume 3: *Rebound From Burnout: Resilience Skills for Ministers.*
Available at www.createspace.com/3854604. This book equips ministers with resilience skills (physical, emotional, and spiritual resilience) to prevent and recover from burnout.

Volume 4: *Transforming Personality: Spiritual Formation and the Five-Factor Model.* Available at www.createspace.com/3925645.
By integrating the spiritual disciplines with assessment tools, this book shows how to use the Five-Factor Personality Model to assess personality, fruit of the Spirit, motivational gifts of the Spirit, ministry aptitudes, vocational aptitudes, and styles of behavior.

Volume 5: *Transforming Shattered Dreams: Hope for Wounded Parents in Global Service.* Available at www.createspace.com/4216990.
This book provides hope for parents of prodigal children.

Volume 6: *Rebound From Crisis: Resilience for Crisis Survivors.*
Available at www.createspace.com/3935466. This book provides the same resilience skills as Volume 3. However, Volume 6 is designed specifically for church members.

Volume 7: *The New Birth Transition: Conquering Rejection.*
Available at www.createspace.com/4391591. This book provides new Christians with skills to profess their faith in cultures that tend to disdain Christians.

Volume 8: *Abusive Power: When Christians Hurt Other Christians.*
Available at www.createspace.com/4796808. This book helps Christians recover from abusive power-based behaviors of others.

Abusive Power:

When Christians Hurt

Other Christians

The Living Well Series, Volume 8

Nathan Davis

Chapter photos by iStockphoto and Photobucket.

ISBN-13: 978-1499386929

ISBN-10: 1499386923

Printed in USA

Dedication

To Cary Tidwell (1945-2013)

 Cary Tidwell served as a foreign missionary for 40 years. He believed in justice and mercy (kindness). At times his kindness meant that he kept a candy dish on his desk for others to enjoy, though he seldom ate it himself. At other times he showed up with pastries for a meeting when he had no plans of sharing in the indulgence. He made endless trips to the airport for friends and colleagues. Frequently, he stayed after meetings to clean up after others. As a leader, no ministry role seemed too menial for him. After retirement, he volunteered as the office manager at my office, and spent extra hours cleaning the building and taking out the trash.

Cary pursued justice by encouraging communication between individuals whenever he saw a potential for conflict. Not everyone agreed with him, but he continued to pursue dialog.

This book makes the point that the degree to which Christians serve others with justice and mercy (kindness) possibly acts as a primary indicator of spiritual maturity. Along with many others, I miss Cary. However, his model of pursing justice and serving with kindness will continue to have an impact on the way we live our lives.

Table of Contents

Preface for Case Studies

The details of the case studies in this book are greatly abbreviated to include only the facts related to power and control. Each case study represents a real incident *as perceived* by one or two participants. However, the perceptions may or may not accurately or completely represent all the facts. For the purposes of this book, the facts remain less important than the perceptions—abuse results from the individual's perceptions, not the facts.

The names of all the case study participants have been changed to fictitious names, i.e., pastor John, pastor David, and pastor Thomas. Any association of these names to actual individuals represents mere coincidence.

CHAPTER 1

Some Christians Abuse Power

Recently, a group of churches in a well-known denomination split away and formed a new church denomination. A few months later on the other side of the world, a sister church denomination split in half. In each case, the splinter group retained the same doctrinal truths as their mother group. So from all appearances, neither split occurred over an issue of theology, but very probably over the issue of power and control. Many non-Christians seem puzzled by the proliferation of church denominations with little or no theological differences. The hidden issue of power and control possibly causes more dissension between Christians and within a church denomination than all other issues combined.

Power, control, and authority exists in every organization, and are needed for the efficiency and welfare of the organization and it's members. To further the personal power of an individual, sometimes a member tries to exploit the power of others, abusing a desirable organizational attribute for the member's own self-serving purpose.

Case Study #1:

A newly appointed missionary couple moved overseas with great expectations. Toward the end of their first term, they dreamed of planting an evangelistic center in a major city that would serve the entire country. Their mid-level supervisor supported them, and their stateside headquarters approved the project for presentation at the next national convention. The presentation raised a large amount of funds. However, the leadership in the foreign country objected to the project because they were not included in the decision making process.

When the missionary couple returned to the States for a furlough, they traveled extensively for two years to continue raising funds for the evangelistic center. Upon arrival in their country of service, however, they felt shocked to discover that the funds had been used to finance the ministry projects of other pastors. Apparently, the local leadership had failed to include the missionary couple or their mid-level supervisor in discussions about redirecting the funds toward other projects.

As a result of the above incident:

1. The missionary couple transferred to another country.
2. What appeared as unethical behavior in the local leadership led the missionary's children to distrust ministers.

Definition

In this book, power-based abuse is defined as any act that promotes the status, dominance, authority, or identity of an individual or organization at the expense of the status, dominance, authority, or identity of others. Most often, the abuse initiates secretly without the input or consent of the victim. Thus, power-based abuse always occurs at the expense of others, and usually without their consent or input.

The consent and input condition seems crucial. By joining an organization, I automatically give management consent to make numerous decisions that affect me without my input or consent. So a fine line may exist between an acceptable use of power, versus the abuse of power.

In ministry, Christians make numerous decisions that affect others. Since we cannot obtain the consent and input of every individual affected by every decision, we inevitably:

1. Unintentionally make decisions that may appear abusive.
2. Make a decision that abuses a minority but still helps the majority.
3. Make a decision that abuses a majority but still helps the organization.

When (not if) the above occurs, two factors seem crucial:

1. The intent to harm
2. The expectations of the victim

Although natural disasters and accidents injure people, the most devastating emotional injury occurs when someone intends to inflict harm. That is, the perception of intent greatly increases the emotional impact of the injury. For instance, I may feel little emotional injury if a distracted automobile driver almost hits me in a cross-walk. However, I will feel much more emotional injury if someone intentionally pushes me into the path of an oncoming automobile. Intent makes a difference. Most victims recover more quickly then they perceive no intent to harm.

Expectations also make a difference. We expect intentional injury from enemies. But since we expect Christians to value justice and kindness, abuse is all the more hurtful when it comes from them. I hardly feel a twinge of anger as a third-world child tries to steal my wallet, but I feel outrage if a religious leader tries to swindle or manipulate me with a power-based move. So as we put peers, pastors, missionaries, and evangelists on a pedestal of near-perfect saint-hood, our expectations of them rises to a level where their acts can cause more harm than they ever intended.

The Apostles as well as many others tried to put Jesus on a pedestal as king. Instead, Jesus rejected the pedestal and modeled the life of a servant.

We expect kindness and mercy from parents, Christians, and religious leaders. When we find them intentionally abusing us in the face of our opposite expectation, recovery seems difficult.

Abusive behavior is only part of the problem. The inflated expectations of the victim sometimes function to increase the severity of the harm. Although this seems like blaming the victim for the abuse, it offers great hope for recovery. The victim controls his or her own expectations. Recovery begins by making sense of the abuse. Chapter 4 presents a structure for this process, which is called reframing.

Power-Based Symptoms

Common symptoms that may indicate a culture of power-based exploitation in a church organization include:

1. Hidden or secretive meetings that neglect to include input or consent from those affected by the meetings
2. Input solicited only as a ploy to gain acceptance from the members (the final decision has already been made)
3. Bullying—acts that neglect justice or kindness in the pursuit of dominance and control
4. Acts that discredit the competence of others, steal credit, or spread rumors
5. Acts that socially or financially isolate others
6. Acts of manipulation instead of dialog

7. Large amounts of energy spent on protecting or advancing the status of an individual

8. A wake of hurt peers and subordinates

9. Dismantling—instead of building on the prior accomplishments of others, the power-based Christian systematically dismantles the achievements and organizational structures of those he or she replaces.

10. Cronyism—acts in which the incoming pastor or authority figure automatically replaces previous staff members with personal friends.

Most of the above symptoms require no explanation, and the negative impact on the church organization seems almost self-evident. However, many individuals fail to recognize acts characterized by manipulation or cronyism.

Acts of Manipulation

The Mirriam-Webster Dictionary (2014) provides several definitions of manipulation:

1. to manage or utilize skillfully

2. to control or play upon by artful, unfair, or insidious means especially to one's own advantage

3. to change by artful or unfair means so as to serve one's purpose

The first definition shows that skillful and clever acts of manipulation may or may not include dishonesty. For instance, parents may try to manipulate their child to study. A physician may try to manipulate a patient to adopt a healthy diet. An employer may try to manipulate a good worker to remain employed at the present job instead of working elsewhere. Ministers may try to manipulate non-Christians to believe in the Gospel, and try to manipulate their members to grow spiritually. Skillful and healthy manipulation occurs with effective parenting, employee management, medical intervention, and pastoring.

However, ministers sometimes grow so accustomed to healthy forms of manipulation that they succumb to power-based manipulation. That is, they cease to function as a servant and pursue self-serving manipulation. Power-based manipulation occurs when an individual promotes the status, dominance, authority, or identity of him/herself or organization *at the expense of* the status, dominance, authority, or identity of others. When the above acts function *at the expense of* others, they become unloving, un-Christ-like, dishonest, and exploitive. If you feel like someone is trying to manipulate you, they almost certainly are. A key to recognizing power-based manipulation lies with the lack of open and thorough dialog. If you cannot discuss a topic openly, power-based manipulation most likely exists. Since power-based manipulation remains inherently hidden, church organizations seldom take notice of it.

Power-based manipulation almost always uses passive-aggressive methods. The Mayo clinic defines passive-aggressive behavior as, "a pattern of indirectly expressing negative feelings instead of openly addressing them. There's a disconnect between what a passive-aggressive person says and what he or she does" (2014). Although most Christians easily recognize aggressive behavior, passive-aggressive behavior is much more difficult to recognize.

Passive-Aggressive Behaviors

According to Simon (2000), the unhealthy forms of manipulation (see power-based symptom 6, above) often implement the following passive-aggressive behaviors:

1. Lying by omission—a subtle form of lying by withholding a significant amount of the truth. This form of manipulation also affects power-based symptoms 1, 2, 4, and 10 above.

2. Denial—manipulator refuses to admit that he or she has done something wrong. This form of manipulation usually affects power-based symptom 3, above.

3. Rationalization—an excuse made by the manipulator for inappropriate behavior. Rationalization often includes "spin" that affects power-based symptoms 4, 8, 9, and 10 above.

4. Minimization—a denial coupled with rationalization. The manipulator asserts that his or her behavior is less harmful than suggested. For example, minimizing a taunt or insult as only a joke.

5. Selective inattention or selective attention—the manipulator refuses to pay attention to anything that may distract from his or her agenda, saying things like "I don't want to hear it".

6. Diversion—steering the conversation onto another topic.

7. Intimidation—manipulator uses veiled (subtle, indirect or implied) threats.

8. Guilt—a manipulator suggests that the victim does not care enough, is too selfish or has it easy.

9. Playing the victim—a manipulator acts as a victim of circumstance or of someone else's behavior to gain pity and compassion and thereby get something from another.

10. Defaming the victim—related to symptom 4, above.

11. Playing the servant role—cloaking a self-serving agenda in the guise of a service to a more noble cause.

12. Seduction—manipulator uses charm, flattery or overtly supports others to gain their trust and loyalty. Friendliness and helpfulness always remain appropriate. However, using charm and flattery simply to further a personal agenda remains deceptive.

13. Feigning innocence—a manipulator suggests that any harm was unintentional or that they never performed the act of which they were accused.

Aggressive Behaviors

According to Simon (2000), the unhealthy forms of manipulation may include the following aggressive behaviors:

1. Blaming
2. Anger—used to shock the victim into submission
3. Shaming—sarcasm and insults used to increase fear and self-doubt in the victim

Cronyism

Cronyism represents favoritism toward personal friends over those who show merit and effective performance. In some church organizations, cronyism shows itself when the new pastor or authority figure automatically replaces previous staff members with personal friends. As the saying goes, "It's not what you know but who you know," or, as blogger Danny Ferguson put it, "It's not what you don't know; it's who your college roommate knows." The U.S. government has outlawed this practice for civil service employees since 1883. They recognized the loss of skills, loss of productivity, and demoralization caused by cronyism. The Los Angeles Times (May 7, 2014) reports a more recent incident in which the Thailand court ousted their prime minister after an abuse-of-power verdict, "Shinawatra's opponents had accused her of transferring the official National Security Council head in order to install a member of her influential family in that post." Thus, she lost her position as prime minister due to cronyism.

Wikipedia (2014) states the following about cronyism:

The economic and social costs of cronyism are paid by society. Those costs are in the form of reduced business opportunity for the majority of the population, reduced competition in the market place, inflated consumer goods prices, decreased economic performance, inefficient business investment cycles, reduced motivation in affected organizations, and the diminution of economically productive activity. A practical cost of cronyism manifests in the poor workmanship of public and private community projects. Cronyism is self-perpetuating; cronyism then begets a culture of cronyism. This can only be apprehended by a comprehensive, effective, and enforced legal code, with empowered government agencies which can effect prosecutions in the courts. In general, authoritarian and totalitarian regimes are more vulnerable to acts of cronyism simply because the officeholders are not accountable, and all office holders generally come from a similar background.

To translate the above Wikipedia statement about secular cronyism into a description for church organizations:

The economic and spiritual costs of cronyism are paid by the church. These costs are in the form of reduced ministry opportunities in the community, reduced quality in the ministerial staff, decreased ministry performance, ineffective ministry outreaches, reduced motivation, and less growth. Cronyism results in a reduced quality of ministry.

Since office holders in church organizations come from a similar background (ministers), church organizations are particularly vulnerable to cronyism. Unless specific boundaries make office holders accountable for cronyism, the church organization may grow a culture of cronyism. The individual who champions cronyism can always find reasons to rationalize the appointment of a friend. Therefore, once a culture of cronyism exists, it almost always persists indefinitely until legislation and regulations impose a system based on merit. So churches that function autonomously from their parent denomination possibly suffer the most from cronyism—they lack accountability.

Leadership certainly possesses the right to replace workers. However, cronyism represents the lack of justice (merit performance ceases to count), the lack of mercy (cronyism results in a lack of kindness toward the individual replaced by someone else), the avoidance of dialog, and the abuse of power. Many organizations call this the "good-ol-boy" style of management. Ministers sometimes fear a lack of loyalty more than a lack of skills. So they succumb to cronyism in order to secure loyalty.

Cronyism may comply with local employment laws, but often uses insensitive, unloving, and un-Christ-like behavior that demoralizes workers and ministers. Fairness represents one of the most basic ethical themes. As stated by Aristotle, "Equals should be treated equally and unequals unequally." Cronyism interferes with fairness because it gives undue advantage to someone based on their relationship instead of their merit or performance. Many pagan countries like Thailand recognize cronyism as an unethical practice, and outlaw it. Yet, some church organizations accept it without question.

Exercise 1-1:

1. What power-based symptoms are evident in your organization (see page 4)?

2. What are some ways that manipulation occurs in your organization (see page 6)?

3. What are some evidences of cronyism in your organization (see page 8)?

4. List the symptoms of power and control (see page 4) in case study #1.

5. The couple in case study #1 chose to transfer to another country. What possible opportunities were lost with that choice?

6. Instead of transferring to another country, what other choices might be worth considering?

CHAPTER 2

Myths About Power and Control

Five Church Myths about Power

Some churches, religious organizations, and individuals accept or promote myths that enable and even encourage power-based exploitation. When victims of abuse can participate in eliminating these myths, they tend to recover more quickly.

The following myths can promote power-based exploitation in your church organization:

1. *Myth—Since power-based exploitation represents the norm for secular culture and business, it represents acceptable behavior in the church.* Truth—Christians look to the Bible for acceptable behavior norms, not culture or business norms. The Bible promotes servant-hood rather than ladder climbing. Jesus avoided power even when secular society wanted to make Him king. Instead, He modeled washing feet, including

the feet of the person soon to betray Him. Instead of insensitivity, the Good Samaritan invites us to mercy and kindness.

2. *Myth—If God allows power-based* exploitation, *it must represent His will in that instance.* Truth—God allows Satan to rule the earth and allows all type of sin in the world. The sin and carnality in this world never represents God's will. Just as He allowed the tribes of Israel to worship idols, He allows men today to pursue and worship the idols of power and control, even as He grieves their choice.

3. *Myth—Trying to oppose a power-based leader is unchristian.* Truth—The Apostle Paul opposed the Apostle Peter's position on dietary laws for Gentiles. Thus, the biblical example promotes dialog during a disagreement, not automatic surrender to someone in a position of power. Manmade rules which expect or require surrender circumvent the example of the Apostle Paul. Paul demonstrates that dialog often identifies a more godly solution. When power or control cultures dictate automatic surrender, the culture remains secular, and based in preserving the existing power structure. A position of power or authority rarely over-rules the need for dialog.

4. Myth—*It is acceptable for a leader to injure others with power-based behavior because God placed the leader in position.* Truth—A leadership position may or may not represent God's blessing. God allows carnal and sinful pursuits, even by His followers. So some Christian leaders attain positions of power through carnal motives, and some attain positions of power due to God's will. The pursuit of

carnality never represents His will, but represents what He allows Christians to choose. God allows carnal Christians to operate in accordance with their carnality.

5. *Myth—If a power-based individual is doing good work, injuring others is acceptable.* Truth—The behavior of the priest or Levite in the Good Samaritan story remains a sin regardless of their good work or religious status. Matthew 23:23 sums up God's desire, "But you have neglected the more important matters of the law—justice, mercy, and faithfulness." Thus, working for God never justifies injuring others by neglecting justice and mercy.

Davis (2012), found that only 9% of the missionaries in her church denomination agreed with myth #5. However, belief in the myths changed dramatically as a function of the region in which the missionaries serve. For instance, in one particular region, 81% of missionaries accepted myth #5. Any single myth enables power-based abuse. If your church organization acts prejudicial against those who object to any of these myths, it probably promotes a culture of power and control.

Secular Myths about Power and Control

Many secular organizations condone and sometimes even promote the abuse of power in the workplace. In his best-selling book, *The 48 Laws of Power*, Robert Green (2000) describes 48 laws that promote the use of power in the workplace. Most of the laws directly contradict Scripture. Possibly the book attained best seller status because so many North Americans desire power, and fail to recognize the spiritual implications of secular power-based "laws." When Christians adopt the common secular myths below, they inevitably fail to engage in healthy dialog, and act insensitively toward others.

Ten Laws (from *The 48 Laws of Power*, Robert Green, 2000) that encourage distrust, deception, and manipulation:

Law #2—Never put too much trust in friends, learn how to use enemies.

Law #3—Conceal your intentions.

Law #4—Always say less than necessary.

Law #7—Get others to do the work for you: but always take the credit.

Law #12—Use selective honesty and generosity to disarm your victim.

Law #14—Pose as a friend, work as a spy.

Law #30—Make your accomplishments seem effortless.

Law #32—Play to peoples fantasies.

Law #38—Think as you like but behave like others.

Law #45—Preach the need for change, but never reform too much at once.

In contrast to the above myths, the Bible says—"Do not steal. Do not lie. Do not deceive one another" Lev. 19:11). "Love does not delight in evil but rejoices with the truth" (1 Cor. 13:6). "Live as children of the light (for the fruit of the light consists in all goodness, righteousness and truth) and find out what pleases the Lord" (Eph. 5:9-10). Be devoted to one another in love. Honor one another above yourselves" (Rom. 12:10). "Submit to one another out of reverence for Christ" (2 Cor. 13:12). "Keep on loving one another as brothers and sisters" (Heb. 13:1). "Love does not delight in evil but rejoices with the truth. It always protects, always trusts, always hopes, always perseveres" (1 Corinthians 13:6-8). "You have heard that it was said, 'Love your neighbor[a] and hate your enemy.' But I tell you, love your enemies and pray for those who persecute you" (Matt 5:43-44).

13 Laws (from *The 48 Laws of Power*, Robert Green, 2000) that build self-pride:

Law #5—So much depends on reputation—guard it with your life.

Law #6—Court attention at all cost.

Law #8—Make other people come to you—use bait if necessary.

Law #22—Use the surrender tactic, transform weakness into power.

Law #26—Keep your hands clean (sic: avoid working in a lowly position).

Law #27—Play on peoples need to believe: create a cult-like following.

Law #31—Control the options: get others to play with the cards you deal.

Law #34—Be royal in your own fashion: act like a king to be treated like one.

Law #37—Create compelling spectacles.

Law #40—Despise the free lunch.

Law #46—Never appear too perfect.

Law #47—Do not go past the mark you aimed for: in victory learn when to stop.

Law #48—Assume formlessness (adapt to your enemy).

In contrast to the above myths, the Bible says—Christians assume the form of a servant. "Be completely humble and gentle; be patient bearing with one another in love" (Eph. 4:2). "The greatest among you will be your servant" (Matt. 23:11).

Five Secular Myths (from *The 48 Laws of Power*, Robert Green, 2000) that promote insensitivity, uncaring, and prejudice

Law #10—Infection: avoid the unhappy and unlucky.

Law #11—Learn to keep people dependent on you.

Law #39—Stir up waters to catch fish.

Law #42—Strike the shepherd and the sheep will scatter.

Law #44—Disarm and infuriate with the mirror effect.

In contrast to the above myths, the Bible says—"I appeal to you, brothers and sisters, in the name of our Lord Jesus Christ, that all of you agree with one another in what you say and that there be no divisions among you, but that you be perfectly united in mind and thought" (1 Cor. 1:10). "Be at peace with each other" (Mark 9:50). See the Good Samaritan story (Luke 10: 25-35).

Nine Laws (from *The 48 Laws of Power*, Robert Green, 2000) that destroy harmony:

Law #15—Crush your enemy totally.

Law #17—Keep others in suspended terror, cultivate an air of unpredictability.

Law #19—Know who you're dealing with—do not offend the wrong person.

Law #16—Use absence to increase respect and honor.

Law #20—Do not commit to anyone.

Law #21—Play a sucker to catch a sucker—seem dumber than your mark.

Law #23—Concentrate you forces.

Law #24—Play the perfect courtier.

Law #33—Discover each man's thumbscrew.

In contrast to the above myths, the Bible says—"Finally, all of you be likeminded, be sympathetic, love one another, be compassionate and humble" (1 Pet. 3:8). "Bear with each other and forgive one another is any of you has a grievance against someone. Forgive as the Lord forgave you." (Col 3: 13). "Live in harmony with one another. Do not be proud, but be willing to associate with people of low position. Do not be conceited" (Rom. 12:16). "But encourage one another daily, as long as it is called 'Today,' so that none of you may be hardened by sin's deceitfulness" (Heb. 3: 13). "And let us consider how we may spur one another on toward love and good deeds, not giving up meeting together, as some are in the habit of doing, but encouraging one another—and all the more as you see the Day approaching" (Heb. 10:24-25). "Be at peace with each other" (Mark 9:50). "Carry each other's burdens, and in this way you will fulfil the law of Christ" (Gal. 6:2). "Live in harmony with one another. Do not be proud, but be willing to associate with people of low position. Do not be conceited" (Rom. 12:16). See the Good Samaritan story.

Two Laws (from *The 48 Laws of Power*, Robert Green, 2000) that promote an atmosphere of fear:

Law #1—Never outshine the master.

Law #41—Avoid stepping into a great man's shoes.

In contrast to the above myths, the Bible says—"There is no fear in love. But perfect love drives out fear, because fear has to do with punishment" (1 Jn. 4:18). These myths are based in a fear that the master will react negatively to a subordinate outshining him or her. While some leaders react negatively to successful subordinates, Scripture urges Christians (including subordinates) to act out of love, not fear. A subordinate who excels as a servant (humbly and with humility) rejects living out of fear. Additionally, success comes from the Lord. "Be completely humble and gentle; be patient bearing with one another in love" (Eph. 4:2). "The greatest among you will be your servant" (Matt.

23:11).

Law #9—Win through your actions, never through argument.

Biblical truth—Christians use all means, including argument. "To the weak I became weak, to win the weak. I have become all things to all people so that by all possible means I might save some" (1 Corinthians 9:22).

Law #13—When asking for help, appeal to people's self-interest, never to their mercy or gratitude.

Biblical truth—Jesus said, "But you have neglected the more important matters of the law—justice, mercy, and faithfulness" (Matthew 23:23).

Seven Laws (from *The 48 Laws of Power*, Robert Green, 2000) that contain truth:

Law #18—Do not build fortresses to protect yourself—isolation is dangerous.

Law #25—Re-create yourself.

Law #28—Enter action with boldness.

Law #29—Plan all the way to the end.

Law #35—Master the art of timing.

Law #36—Disdain things you cannot have: ignoring them is the best revenge.

Law #43—Work on the hearts and minds of others.

Warning—The following case study represents a real incident as perceived by a victim, but the perceptions may or may not accurately or completely represent all the facts.

Case Study #2:

A past denomination leader (pastor John) decided to run once again for a leadership position in his church denomination. He contacted many low income pastors in his denomination and agreed to personally fund their hotel accommodations if they would attend and vote at the national meeting. Since pastor John was running for an elected position, his offer caused a conflict of interest for these pastors (see Power-Based Symptoms 1, 6, and 10).

When the presiding leader (pastor Thomas) learned of this tactic, he publicly denounced "vote buying," cronyism, and corruption in the denomination (see Power-Based Symptoms 3, 4, 5, and 6). Then he published a new written agreement denouncing corruption and required all the existing denomination leaders to publicly sign and support the agreement (see Power-Based Symptoms 3, 4, 5, and 6). Almost everyone saw this reaction as a power-based attempt to publicly humiliate pastor John. Pastor Thomas won the election for the leadership position. However, pastor John won the position as his assistant. The public humiliation also polarized the pastor John supporters against pastor Thomas.

A few months later, pastor Thomas dismissed the denomination's treasurer (one of the pastor John supporters) for moral failure. Before his name was removed from the list of bank signatories for the denomination, however, the dismissed treasurer secretly presented the bank with a group of pastor John supporters and claimed that they now represented the entire denomination (see Power-Based Symptoms 1, 3, 5, 6, and 10). Since no one had yet informed the bank of the treasurer's dismissal, the bank still recognized him as the official treasurer and agreed to change the list of signatories for the denomination. The new signatories pledged allegiance to pastor John as their new denomination leader, blocked pastor Thomas and his supporters from accessing the denomination's funds, and started to spread rumors through the internet about pastor

Thomas (see Power-Based Symptoms 4, 6, 8, and 10). Pastor Thomas and the churches supported by him filed a law suit against the bank. The bank froze all funds pending the outcome of the court case. The church denomination split, some supporting pastor John and some supporting pastor Thomas. Pastor John isolated himself with close friends, and refused to interact with pastor Thomas or his supporters. Churches supporting pastor Thomas started receiving threats from pastor John supporters. Both factions retained identical doctrinal truths.

Reflection 1-3:

1. This case initiated with a public humiliation of pastor John.

2. Although numerous symptoms of power and control (see page 8) exist in this story, acts of manipulation (Power-Based Symptom 6) and cronyism (Power-Based Symptom 10) seem evident throughout most of the events. The manipulation included power-based tactics to overcome the initial shame of pastor John. Pastor John used cronyism when he offered to pay the lodging for disadvantaged pastors, and again when he isolated himself with close friends after the election.

3. The manipulation included at least eight of the thirteen passive-aggressive behaviors listed above: 1, 2, 3, 7, 9, 10, 11, and 12.

4. Many laws from *The 48 Laws of Power* (Robert Green, 2000) seem probable in the story. Six of the Ten Laws that encourage distrust, deception, and manipulation (laws 2, 3, 4, 7, 12, and 14) seem probable. Two of the Five Laws that promote insensitivity, uncaring, and prejudice (laws 11 and 42) seem probable. Five of the Nine Laws that destroy harmony (laws 15, 17, 23, 24, and 33) seem probable.

5. Thus, the secular culture of the community around the church seems to promote at least 13 of the laws promoted by *The 48 Laws of Power*.

6. The denomination may expect similar events in the future until they address the secular myths and a culture of manipulation and cronyism.

Exercise 2-1:

When the incumbent leader (pastor Thomas) heard of pastor John's actions that produced a conflict of interest, pastor Thomas publicly denounced "vote buying," cronyism, and corruption in the denomination (see Power-Based Symptoms 3, 4, 5, and 6), leading to the public humiliation of pastor John. Instead of implementing the above actions to eliminate pastor John's chance of re-election, what might have happened if pastor Thomas:

1. Issued a written reprimanded of pastor John, privately, for unethical conduct, and asked leadership to remove his name from the ballot?

2. Suspended pastor John's credentials for 30 days for unethical conduct (or until after the election)?

3. Followed a more private pathway that avoided public shame while still removing pastor John from the ballot?

Reflections:

1. What topics and past incidents seem off limits to discuss in your church organization? Is there a possibility that power-based manipulation prevents this discussion?

2. What power-based exploitation have you observed in your church denomination?

3. What power-based exploitation have you observed in your circle of Christian friends?

4. Which of Robert Green's 48 laws of power seem accepted within your church denomination? Were the laws promoted by an individual or by your denomination?

5. Which of Robert Green's 48 laws of power seem acceptable at face value until you reflect on them more deeply?

6. To reduce cronyism, consider the following strategies:

   • Limit the number of terms for denomination officials.

   • Limit the length of terms.

   • Develop position papers that define cronyism as unethical, and provide common examples of cronyism.

   • Define cronyism as unethical in the denomination standard of conduct regulations.

   • Teach ministers about cronyism in continuing education and continuing training programs.

7. To reduce unethical behavior at the organizational level, consider the following strategies:

   • Require newly elected leaders to participate in an introductory leadership course within their first two-weeks of office. The course would help elected leaders to set up moral and ethical boundaries related to their leadership role (e.g., handling of funds, gender boundaries, cronyism, property titles, fraternization, etc.) and help them replace secular leadership styles with Biblical leadership styles appropriate to their office.

   • Develop position papers that explicitly define unethical behaviors, and provide common examples of the behaviors.

CHAPTER 3

The Deadliest Sin for Christians?

The Relationship of Power and Control to Envy

Because Christians and ministers want to further the Kingdom of God, they naturally seek a meaningful ministry. Although the quest for a meaningful ministry is highly desirable, it includes two inherent risks:

1. Some people believe that higher levels of power and control will guarantee meaningful ministry. These individuals seek positions or power and control. Woe to those who threaten their power or control, even inadvertently.

2. Some people believe that a more meaningful ministry is available through the pursuit of the ministry roles held by others. These individuals strive to take over the ministry positions and roles held by others, using power and control methods.

Both groups fail to find meaningfulness, and suffer from an insidious form of envy. Meaningful ministry takes place as the individual seeks to serve others—taking on the role of a servant. So those who seek to expand their power or who try to take over the positions of others engage in behaviors exactly the opposite from a role as a servant. They confuse the pride of secular success with meaningful ministry. And their behavior often hurts other Christians.

Pride results when we gain something that we first envied. Thus pride results from envy. For instance, early in my Air Force career, I envied a large plantation style home south of town. Over a period of ten years, I bought land and built an even nicer home of my own. When completed, I felt immense pride in my "mansion." That pride resulted from attaining something which I envied. Although all forms of pride may not include sin (James 1:9), Scripture consistently defines pride in human accomplishments to sin. Proverbs 8:13 says, "To fear the Lord is to hate evil; I hate pride and arrogance, evil behavior and perverse speech." When I first realized that God hates pride, I knew that I needed to sell my house. But God never limits His hate to a pride in material possessions. Just as God hates pride in material possessions, He also hates pride in immaterial possessions such as pride in a ministry role or ministry accomplishments. He hates pride wherever it occurs.

For ministers, envy sometimes shows up in unique ways. When their income remains too meager to hoard material possessions, they sometimes substitute material envy with an envy of power, position, territory, and control (sometimes represented by status and authority). Although the Ten Commandments condemn envy, few sermons address the desire for power and control as a fundamental outcome of envy. When Christians fail to identify their desire for power as a component of envy, they are prone to match their values with the power pursuits of the secular world.

Do Christians Envy?

Over the period of 1998 to 2003, a Five-Factor model of personality assessment was administered to ministers from three different church denominations and one interdenominational group. The comprehensive personality assessment included responses to the following sentences and adjectives about envy:

Jealous

Envious

I am jealous of others who get what I would like to have.

I resent it when I don't get my way.

I get very upset when I am criticized.

Each subject indicated the extent to which the above adjectives characterized him or her, and the extent to which they agreed or disagreed with each of the above sentences. Figure 1 shows the scale used for adjectives, and Figure 2 shows the scale used for sentences.

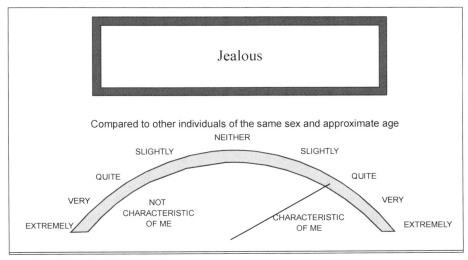

Figure 1: Scale to present adjectives

The subjects moved a mouse cursor to the appropriate position on the arched scale and pressed the mouse button to record the response. The computer actually recorded 45 positions, rather than the 9 which are defined on each scale. The minister's results were compared to the North American norm reported by Christal, R. E. (1994).

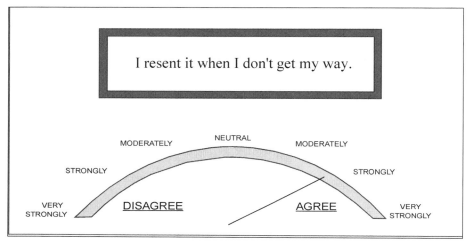

Figure 2: Scale to present sentences

After reflecting on how you typically feel about yourself and your ministry relationships, you may use the same scales to mark your responses to the above adjectives and sentences. Mark the adjective scale (Figure 1) to indicate how characteristic or uncharacteristic each of the above adjectives represents you as compared with other individuals of your same sex and approximate age. Then, mark the sentence scale (Figure 2) to indicate how much you agree or disagree with each of the above sentences. After marking your response to each adjective or sentence, mark the approximate average of your scores on each scale.

When answering the above list of adjective and sentences using the scales in Figures 1 and 2, the average North American responds as *slightly not characteristic* on the adjective scale and as *moderately disagree* on the sentence scale. So if your average score was close to *slightly not characteristic* or *moderately disagree* on each scale, you scored an average amount of envy in comparison to the North American norm. Figures 3 and 4, below, show the North American average in units of standard deviation. The value of zero (0) standard deviations represents the North American norm.

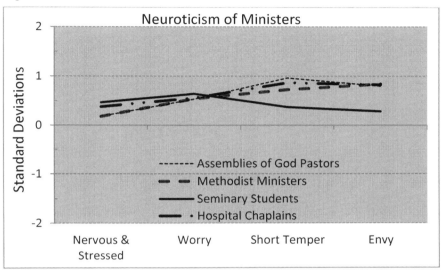

Figure 3: Neuroticism scores for four groups of ministers

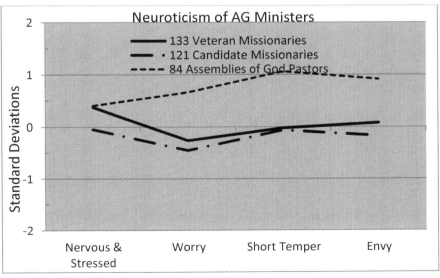

Figure 4: Neuroticism scores for three groups of Assemblies of God ministers

Figures 3 and 4 show the results of envy assessments for each group of ministers. Since the 0 point on the standard deviations scale represents the norm for all North Americans, the envy scores in Figures 3 and 4 indicate that envy may affect clergy (Methodist, Baptist, hospital chaplains, and Assemblies of God pastors) at least as much and possibly even more than the average North American (non-clergy). That is, every ministerial group studied, except foreign missionaries, scored significantly higher on a z-test (p=.05) for the trait of Envy than the North American norm (Davis, 2012). However, even missionaries scored an average amount of Envy compared to the North American norm.

Some individuals feel discouraged when they see their envy score as average or above average. After all, almost every Christian expects positive results for traits related to spiritual growth. However, every individual possesses one or more negative traits that relate to spiritual growth. A comprehensive assessment provides an indication of potential growth areas. Research indicates that envy scores change dramatically as a function of practicing some of the spiritual disciplines (see Chapter 7 in *Transforming Personality: Spiritual Formation and the Five-Factor Model.*, Davis, 2012).

Galatians 5:19-20 states, "The acts of the flesh are obvious: sexual immorality, impurity and debauchery; idolatry and witchcraft; hatred, discord, jealousy, fits of rage, selfish ambition, dissensions, factions and envy; drunkenness, orgies, and the like." Of the above acts, the Five-Factor Model directly assesses several carnal traits including envy. When ministers show as much or more envy than the average North American who may or may not follow Jesus, the ministers may offer a poor example to non-Christians, and easily fall into a habit of power-based abuse.

What Does the Bible Say About Envy?

In the Garden of Eden, Satan tempted Adam and Eve to envy God. When Satan referred to the forbidden fruit, he said to Eve, "For God knows that when you eat of it your eyes will be opened, and you will be like God, knowing good and evil (Gen. 3:5)." Thus, humankind's first sin was possibly not in eating the forbidden fruit, after all; but the first sin involved succumbing to Satan's temptation to envy (to be like) God. The sin that resulted in the fall and expulsion from the Garden of Eden apparently included envy. Adam and Eve envied God. That is, they wanted to be like Him. However, what did they envy about Him? Possibly, power and control. By envying this, they not only refused to submit to Him, they also set up a pattern of seeking power and control above almost everything else. Most Christians easily recognize envy of material possessions but sometimes fail to recognize their envy of immaterial possessions such as power and control.

Envy, however, existed before Adam and Eve's sin. Much earlier, Satan succumbed to envying God. That alone resulted in Satan's fall. So envy seems to act as a primary root of evil, displaying itself as an envy of power and control. When Satan tempted Jesus in the wilderness, he offered all the kingdoms of the world to Jesus. Satan offered power to Jesus if He would, in turn, give more power to Satan by worshiping him (Matt. 4:9). Envy possibly serves as an underlying factor in each of the Ten Commandments (Exod. 20:3-17).

Christians may demonstrate a lifestyle of material simplicity yet seek immaterial possessions like power and control. Self-willed effort is not enough. Engaging in specific spiritual disciplines will actually target the problem of envy.

The Relationship between Envy and Submission

Many issues stimulate conflict between Christians. But when envy stimulates a desire for recognition, power, or authority, it blocks the act of submission and service. The Christian no longer acts as a servant. So when a church faces internal conflict, look for the hidden issue of power and control. Those who envy hidden issues (a desire for recognition, power, and authority) almost always cause a more insidious problem than those who envy material possessions. If the issue of power and control seems to stimulate a conflict in your church work, address that issue before addressing any other.

The level of leadership seems almost irrelevant to the problem of envy. In Matthew 23:23, Jesus sums up the problem, "But you have neglected the more important matters of the law—justice, mercy, and faithfulness." Thus, power hungry Christians tend to exploit and even abuse others, often unintentionally, because they place a higher priority on power-based pursuits than justice, mercy, and faithfulness. They may believe in justice and mercy but simply neglect those values in lieu of their focus on power and control. These Christians may produce a wake of injured individuals as a by-product of pursuing power and control. Leaders and non-leaders alike seem to abuse others when they place their drive for power and control above "the more important matters of the law—justice, mercy, and faithfulness."

These individuals tend to control almost everything. They may expect everyone in a lower position to submit, not realizing that by envying power they lack mutual submission, themselves. They may know that a good leader should empower others by giving away power, but because they envy those with power, they give away work without giving away decision power or authority. For instance, some leaders teach a seminar but avoid training others to reteach the seminar. Or, they may earn an advanced degree, not to increase knowledge, but simply for the position or recognition it brings. Some insist on a title of "Director" even when no one works for them. In one office, Christian workers frequently sought the position of "Team Leader" even when the position merely included accounting duties that they emphatically despised. More damaging quarrels occur over position, power, and territorial disputes, than theology, doctrine, or worship styles.

In a similar pattern to New Testament times, today's Christians sometimes seek power and control more than justice and mercy. And in the same way, pastors and church members alike may overlook or even reject justice and mercy when it threatens their power and control.

Servant-hood results from the freedom of envy (envy of material objects and especially envy of immaterial objects such as power, position, control, care, security, or acceptance). Authentic servant-hood eradicates conspicuous consumption and power-based behaviors. Simplicity results from the lack of envy. That is, envy and the lack thereof act as the causal agent that affects behavior.

The Apostle Paul said, "Do not associate with a greedy man" (1 Cor. 5:11). In Ephesians 5:5, he said, "No immoral, impure, or greedy person—such a man is an idolater—has an inheritance in the Kingdom of Christ and God." As shown in Figures 4 and 5, ministers possibly as much as any other profession, envy power, position, territory, and control even more than material possessions.

Power-Based Exploitation Versus Agreeableness

Power-based exploitation generally includes two character facets associated with the personality trait of *Agreeableness*, (1) a lack of sympathy, and (2) an excess of insensitivity. These character facts enable a power-based individual to pursue self-serving behaviors at the expense of others. And this exploitation meets the power-based definition outlined in page 2 of this book.

Figure 5, below, shows the *Agreeableness* facets for five groups of ministers. A z-test confirms that the scores for veteran AG missionaries, hospital chaplains, and Baptist seminary students are statistically identical to each other. Figure 5 shows that most of the ministers studied possess an average or lower than average level of sympathy, and an average amount of insensitivity.

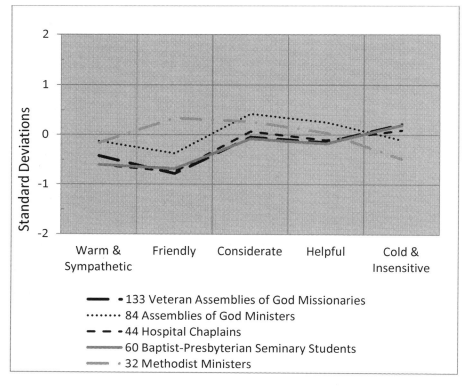

Figure 5: Agreeableness Facets for Five Groups of Ministers

We cannot exactly discern the level of sympathy portrayed by the priest and Levite in the Good Samaritan story (Luke 10: 30-37). However, the story shows these men as unsympathetic and insensitive.

[30] In reply Jesus said: "A man was going down from Jerusalem to Jericho, when he was attacked by robbers. They stripped him of

his clothes, beat him and went away, leaving him half dead. [31] A priest happened to be going down the same road, and when he saw the man, he passed by on the other side. [32] So too, a Levite, when he came to the place and saw him, passed by on the other side. [33] But a Samaritan, as he traveled, came where the man was; and when he saw him, he took pity on him. [34] He went to him and bandaged his wounds, pouring on oil and wine. Then he put the man on his own donkey, brought him to an inn and took care of him. [35] The next day he took out two denarii and gave them to the innkeeper. "Look after him," he said, "and when I return, I will reimburse you for any extra expense you may have."

[36] Which of these three do you think was a neighbor to the man who fell into the hands of robbers? [37] The expert in the law replied, "The one who had mercy on him." Jesus told him, Go and do likewise.

We often try to compare the role of the priest and Levite to present-day Christians and ministers. However, power-based exploitation may illustrate something much more sinister than a lack of sympathy. The basic definition of power-based exploitation (see page 4) includes the condition that the behavior functions *at the expense of* the victim. The exploiter gains more power or control by taking it away from the victim. Some Christians envy the ministry roles of others and try to use power-based tactics to take over their ministry positions. Other Christians simply take power or control away from others. Possibly, the robbers in the Good Samaritan story represent these Christians more accurately than the priest or Levite. After all, the priest and Levite never took anything away from the victim. Thus, power-based exploitation starts with envy and ends with theft.

The Ten Commandments cites envy and theft as sin. Should I turn a blind eye to envy and theft? Do I want to condone a culture that supports the envy and theft of immaterial objects, even when it injures others and sometimes causes others to lose their salvation? I concluded that I hope to avoid looking like the priest, the Levite, and especially the robbers.

Jesus cites an even more sinister reason to avoid the roles of the priest or Levite. Just before telling the story of the Good Samaritan, the Apostle Luke relates the background to the story:

> [25] On one occasion an expert in the law stood up to test Jesus. "Teacher," he asked, "what must I do to inherit eternal life?"
>
> [26] "What is written in the Law?" he replied. "How do you read it?"
>
> [27] He answered, "Love the Lord your God with all your heart and with all your soul and with all your strength and with all your mind; and, 'Love your neighbor as yourself."
>
> [28] "You have answered correctly," Jesus replied. "Do this and you will live."
>
> [29] But he wanted to justify himself, so he asked Jesus, "And who is my neighbor?"

Then, Jesus told the Good Samaritan story. However, the story still follows as an answer to the original question, "what must I do to inherit eternal life?" Some may look at this story as an illustration of "who is my neighbor?" They are dead wrong. The background to the story shows that it further defines "what must I do to inherit eternal life?" With the real question in mind, the roles that we play in the story take on a new significance. If I act like the priest, the Levite, or the robbers, I not only fail to act like a neighbor, but I fail to inherit eternal life.

The previous chapter of this book posed the question, "The deadliest sin for Christians?" While a drive for power and control may or may not serve as the deadliest sin, it possibly serves as the most overlooked.

If you want to discover your personal *Agreeableness* scores, please log onto www.five-factor.com. The assessment is too complex to provide except by computer presentation. However, the assessment is available to everyone, and includes much more information than the *Agreeableness* scores, alone.

Abuse Stimulates Apathy

One of the earliest rigorous studies on church conflict compared three groups from four Methodist congregations that ranged between 400-800 members. John Savage classified the church members into three groups (Savage, 1976):

1. Group A—church members who are active in church
2. Group B—former Group A church members who have become less active in church
3. Group C—former Group B church members who have become completely inactive in church

Savage's research indicates that as church members experience conflict and abuse in their local church, they seem to progressively move from active ministry to less active and eventually to an inactive ministry. Savage found that almost a third (31.2%) of the Group B members reported moderate conflict with the pastor, and over half of the Group "C" members reported significant conflict with the pastor (45.5% reported high conflict and 9% reported moderate conflict). When compared to the 18.8% of Group A members who reported moderate conflict and 4.2% who reported high conflict, the effect of conflict with the pastor seems staggering.

Savage also found that church members seem to conflict with one other even more than they conflict with the pastor. Thus, over a third (35%) of Group B members reported moderate conflict with another church member, and 7% reported high conflict. As conflict intensifies, the members seem to progress from Group B status to Group "C" status.

Thus, 14% of Group "C" reported moderate conflict with another church member, and 32% reported high conflict with another church member. It is reasonable then, to suspect a relationship conflict (abuse) when previously active church members transition to pew-sitters. Savage (56-57) reports, "There appear to be three very significant precipitants to bring these feelings of anxiety. They are in order of their intensity: (1) conflict with the pastor (.001 level of significance), (2) conflict with another family member (.025 level of significance) over church matters, and (3) conflict with another church member (.025 level). In each of the above cases, unresolved personal conflict produces anxiety. These inactive members back off from their church relationships but do not re-engage in any other congregation. They are not church hoppers." Savage concludes, "Both less active and inactive church members showed considerably less ability to cope with conflictual situations" (Savage, 1976, 95). Thus, conflict and abuse play a major role in de-motivating church workers.

Warning—The following case study represents a real incident as perceived by a victim, but the perceptions may or may not accurately or completely represent all the facts.

Case Study #3:

Several pastors served a local church, one as the senior pastor and two as assistant pastors. One of the pastors, pastor David, also served as the treasurer for the entire denomination. While the senior pastor traveled to another country, the denomination revoked pastor David's credentials based on his misuse of funds. It appears that he used denomination funds to help the needy members of his own congregation. Although humiliated by the denomination, the majority of his local church members still loved and supported him. Before the senior pastor could return, pastor David called a secret board meeting composed only of those who supported him (see Power-Based Symptoms 1, 3, 6, and 10). They elected him as the new senior pastor for the church and granted him new credentials issued by the local church. However, a different agency than the local church owned the physical church buildings and property. Also, the church by-laws required that agency to appoint the senior pastor, not the church board. So the agency leaders appointed a different senior pastor (Pastor Thomas) over the local church.

Based on the secret election, Pastor David filed a lawsuit claiming himself and his supporters as the true and rightful owners of the church. He refused to vacate the premises, and formed a new denomination with offices located on the church property (see Power-Based Symptoms 1, 3, 6, 7, and 8). For the most part, the local church members supported his decision to form a new denomination.

Since pastor Thomas lacked support from the local church members and the board members, he resigned. The court sided with the original denomination and agency to award the church property to the agency. Pastor David was removed. Eventually, the local church elected a new senior pastor approved by the agency. The agency donated the buildings and land to the local church.

As a result of the above incidents:

1. Many local pastors grew discouraged and resigned from the ministry.
2. Many church workers and church members stopped attending the local church.
3. The local news media ridiculed the local church and the church denomination.

Case Study Reflection:

1. This case started with a public humiliation of pastor David.
2. Although numerous symptoms of power and control (see page 8) exist in this story, acts of manipulation (Power-Based

Symptom 6) and cronyism (Power-Based Symptom 10) characterize many of the events. The treasurer (pastor David) implemented manipulation and power-based tactics to overcome shame when he lost his credentials. He implemented cronyism when he called a secret election that included only his supporters.

3. The manipulation included at least ten of the thirteen passive-aggressive behaviors listed above: 1, 2, 3, 7, 8, 9, 10, 11, 12, and 13.

4. Five of the Ten Laws that encourage distrust, deception, and manipulation (laws 2, 3, 4, 12, and 14) seem probable. Three of the 13 Laws that build self-pride (laws 6, 27 and 31) seem probable. Two of the Five Laws that promote insensitivity (laws 11 and 39) seem probable. Five of the Nine Laws that destroy harmony (laws 15, 17, 23, 24, and 33) seem probable.

5. Thus, the secular culture of the community around the church seems to promote at least 15 of the laws promoted by *The 48 Laws of Power*.

6. The denomination may expect similar events in the future until they address the probable secular laws and a culture of manipulation and cronyism that has infiltrated their churches.

Exercise 3-1:

What are some symptoms of envy in case study #3?

In hindsight, what are some kindness and mercy based strategies that may have prevented the turmoil of case study #3?

When pastor David lost his credentials, what were some other ways that the denomination could have dismissed him? For instance, could they have delayed the notification until the senior pastor's return, and let him dismiss Pastor David, with a board meeting immediately following to explain the action to the board?

Reflection:

1. Figures 3, 4 and 5 show that some Christians struggle with envy. What is your score for envy? How do you compare to the North American norm?

2. What is your honest appraisal of your level of sympathy in comparison to the average North American?

3. Describe how the traits of *Agreeableness, Sympathy* and *Sensitivity* to others would affect each of the secular 48 laws of power discussed by Robert Green in Chapter 2.

4. Of your past acquaintances who stopped attending church, how many suffered from abuse and conflict?

CHAPTER 4

Overcoming Personal Injury

As long as God uses people to show His love to the world, some will use the organization (church) to further their own base of power and control. That is, they will hold justice and kindness as secondary values to their self-serving interest in power and control. Regardless, power-based exploitation (see definition on page 2) is always inappropriate. God says, "But you have neglected the more important matters of the law—justice, mercy, and faithfulness." So when Christians witness a lack of justice or mercy (kindness), the problem originates in humankind's desires, not God's. He wants justice and kindness.

To the dismay of many, no Christian reaches infallibility this side of heaven. And a few Christians have even blessed me with the knowledge of my personal fallibility—I inadvertently hurt them. To minister as a human, we inevitably hurt other Christians as their expectations collide with our carnal motives. We hardly know our own motives, much less the expectations of others. So conflict is inevitable. The degree to which Christians serve others without hurting them may serve as a reflection of spiritual maturity.

Normal Questions about Power-Based Exploitation

1. Why would a good God allow a power-based Christian to injure me? God allows carnality and bad judgment throughout the world, even among Christians. God never promises to make life on this earth easy, safe, happy, just, or secure. He only promises to be with us, always. He sits with us in the injury, and works in the injury to make something good come from it. However, the "good" may not include justice or mercy on this earth. The "good" on this earth may include nothing more than personal or spiritual growth. From an eternal perspective, nothing else matters.

2. Does my injury from a power-based Christian result as a punishment or part of my destiny? Sometimes bad events happen, not according to any particular plan or according to God's will, but simply by chance, by someone's neglect, or because of someone's carnality. Avoid letting anyone, including yourself, define your injury as a punishment or destiny. Any such designation puts you in the role of God, setting yourself up as a judge of His intentions. Only God knows His intentions. Avoid trying to judge His motives.

3. Why does life feel so meaningless after an abuse? People find meaningfulness in relationships. So when Christians abuse

each other, the relationships sour and they lose a sense of meaningfulness with that individual and with everyone affected by that individual. Recognize the abuse as abnormal. The loss of meaningfulness remains a normal result of abuse. We can continue to build meaningfulness with other people and with God.

Growth Occurs as We Make Sense of Hurts

I have been hurt by Christians. And anyone working in a church more than a few years has probably experienced injury, too. Expectations for a pain-free church environment are unrealistic. Some people languish in pain for a lifetime. Instead of running away or languishing in pain, we possess an option to face it and make sense of it.

A well-known psychologist, Martin Seligman, states (2002, xi), "The positive emotions of confidence, hope, and trust, for example, serve us best not when life is easy, but when life is difficult." So a resilient Christian reframes suffering and uses it to build a more spiritual character. Thus, making sense of a hurt helps each Christian to persevere through the worst of crises. The Apostle Paul states the principle a little more clearly, "And we rejoice in the hope of the glory of God. Not only so, but we also rejoice in our sufferings, because we know that suffering produces perseverance; perseverance, character; and character, hope. And hope does not disappoint us, because God has poured out his love into our hearts by the Holy Spirit, whom he has given us" (Romans 5: 2-5, NIV). Seligman accurately notes that suffering produces perseverance. The Apostle Paul goes several steps further, observing that suffering produces perseverance, perseverance produces character, and character produces more hope.

Another psychologist, Jonathan Haidt, notes a primary function of suffering—humans *need* suffering to produce character. Although Romans 5:2-5 states that suffering produces character and hope, most Christians try their best to avoid it. For example, Christians highly value passing their beliefs onto their children. But how often do parents pray for their children to experience suffering so that they will develop character? Romans states that suffering produces perseverance; perseverance, character; and character, hope. But few believers ask God to send more suffering to stimulate their children's character development. If we really believe Scripture, "We should take more chances and suffer more defeats. It means that we might be dangerously overprotecting our children, offering them lives of bland safety and too much counseling while depriving them of the 'critical incidents' that would help them to grow strong (Haidt, 141)."

Suffering operates as a fundamental component to produce character. As we reflect and make sense of our suffering, we use the worst of life's stressors to build additional character and resilience. And just as we prefer to offer our children lives of bland safety, most of us also prefer that lifestyle for ourselves, rather than the stark reality of what we face. Thus the safely contented and isolated Christian possibly fails to grow. And those who run away and refuse to face their injury also fail to recover a full life.

Helpful Steps for Recovering Christians

Christians cannot avoid pain. However, we can understand and grow from it. To understand and grow from a power-based pain, consider the following five steps:

1. Explain the facts of what happened.
2. Identify your thoughts during the events.
3. Identify your emotions during the events.

4. Dialog with your abuser, if possible.
5. Reframe the events with an eternal-viewpoint instead of an event viewpoint.

Step 1—Explain the Facts

Healing begins as we face and verbally process our pain. Verbalization provides an extremely important intervention—it activates a different part of the brain than used for non-verbal tasks. Verbally describe the facts and events surrounding your pain from your own perspective. Then write a narration of the facts. Specifically describe your role and the top-level facts that occurred sequentially during the incident, such as who did what and when. Start by relating only the top-level facts and sequence of events, without describing your thoughts and emotions. As you start the healing process by narrating only the facts and events, you can feel secure in the knowledge that you can avoid digging into your raw emotions.

Warning—The following case study represents a real incident *as perceived* by a victim, but the perceptions may or may not accurately or completely represent all the facts.

Case Study #4:

Pastor John experienced an incident in which his new senior pastor used a power-based approach to replace him with a personal friend (cronyism). If you have worked in a church organization for very long, you may have experienced something similar:

Following a change in pastoral leadership, the new senior pastor invited a personal friend to visit him. In a staff meeting two days later, the senior pastor suddenly announced that pastor John was immediately replaced with his personal friend, pastor Thomas. To prevent any further discussion, the senior pastor immediately assigned every individual to different teams to discuss some new office procedures, and then disappeared for the remainder of the day.

Notice that the above narration avoids any mention of thoughts or emotions even though pastor John felt plenty of emotions. It focuses merely on the facts and sequence of events that occurred— who did what, when. Once the facts are written in a narrative format, most victims can easily identify the power-based symptoms from page 4, the passive-aggressive acts of manipulation from pages 6 and 8, and the 48 Laws of Power from pages 16-20. For instance, the above narrative describes power-based symptoms 1, 3, 6, 9 and 10 (see page 4). It especially illustrates cronyism. Of the 48 Laws of Power, the senior pastor possibly used 3, 4, 14, 15, 17 and 24.

During this step, some individuals tend to describe their thoughts and feelings. However, try to limit your narration to the facts, only. Without emotion, describe the facts as accurately as you can. Then compare your facts to the list of power-based symptoms on page 4. If you experienced power-based abuse, which power-based symptoms seem evident in your incident? Which passive-aggressive acts from pages 6 and 8 seem evident in your incident? Which of the 48 Laws of Power from pages 16-20 seem evident in your incident?

When a victim experiences multiple incidents, try to describe each incident separately. For instance, some instigators stimulate an environment full of abuse. Narrate the incidents, one day at a time, until you finish describing all the incidents. By describing each day separately, you can keep the facts clearer.

Step 2—Identify Your Thoughts

Describe your thoughts during each part of the incident. Start by recalling the first part of the incident, and try to remember your initial thoughts at each instant. Then mentally proceed slowly through the entire incident, trying to recall your thoughts during each stage. You may recall your thoughts quickly, or you may discover that this is a difficult process. Some individuals simply react with little or no thoughts until the entire incident passes.

Some Christians feel guilty about their automatic thoughts. Remember that the abuse is abnormal, not your automatic thoughts. Your automatic thoughts result as a normal outcome from any stressor. Upon reconsideration, most Christians quickly discard their automatic carnal-based thoughts. Your long-term choice to control your thoughts and tempter helps to consciously edit your automatic thoughts, and enables a more Christ-like response.

Application:

During the above crisis, pastor John described his automatic thoughts as follows:

> I felt like I was losing my identity and meaningfulness in ministry. I knew that I had done an outstanding job in the past, so how could the senior pastor act so unjustly? How could he act so unkindly to do this without any discussion? If he dislikes my work or wants to proceed in a different direction, why didn't he discuss it with me? How can the church board members and other church members support him? Do any of the board members or church members care about me? Can I trust anyone?

Most of pastor John's thoughts formed into questions and negative interpretation due to the lack of dialog. By turning each of your questions into statements, you can sometimes identify your automatic thoughts. For instance,

1. "How can the senior pastor act so unjustly?" became, "He is acting unjustly."
2. "How can he act so unkindly?" became, "He is acting unkindly."
3. "Why hasn't he discussed things with me?" became, "He doesn't value any of my opinions."
4. "How can the board members support him?" became, "The board members do not value me or the work that I have done."
5. "Do any of the board members or church members care about me?" became, "The board members and church members do not care about me."
6. "Can I trust anyone?" became, "I cannot trust anyone anymore."

Please note that many automatic thoughts are false. During the heat of a crisis, we have little control over these thoughts. And when we fail to dialog with others, we tend to believe these thoughts. Thus, almost every individual needs help to assess and refute their automatic thoughts. Find a pastor or two who you trust, or find a counselor to help you with this process. Specifically look for thoughts that include:

Blaming

Overstatements

Mind-reading

Labeling

Imperatives (statements that include "why, should, ought, or must")

Negative interpretation

Fortune telling

To learn more about these thought distortions, please see *Transforming Conflict: Relationship Skills for Ministers*, available at Amazon.com and at www.createspace.com/3856947. Since automatic thoughts spawn from raw emotions, they may or may not represent truthful thinking. Thoroughly discuss your automatic thoughts (like those above) with trusted pastors, peers, or counselors to make sure the thoughts represent reasonable conclusions.   Unfortunately, many Christians and ministers get discouraged and quit functioning in ministry due to their automatic thoughts. They would probably continue working if they tried to discuss the truthfulness of their thoughts with some unbiased friends, pastors, and counselors. Apart from discussing these thoughts with an unbiased pastor or counselor, most individuals find these thoughts extremely difficult to refute.

Step 3—Identify Your Emotions

Identify your feelings during each step of the incident, and immediately afterward. If you find difficulty identifying your feelings during a crisis, consider you surface level feelings and your deeper feelings.

Some surface feelings include:

Unhappy

Envy

Fear

Nervous/Stressed out

Angry/mad

Shame/guilt

Sad

Hurt

Some deep feelings include:

Out of Control

Unrecognized

Unvalued

Unloved

Unappreciated

Unaccepted

Honesty is questioned

Integrity is questioned

Application:

Continuing with the same incident described above, pastor John described his feelings as follows:

Naturally, I felt unhappy. However, I also felt fear because my senior pastor avoided and seemed to actively prevent any dialog. Thus, I didn't know where I stood with him except that he wanted me replaced, and it seemed that no one cared. I felt shame and hurt since he announced his discussion publically without any prior input or warning. For deeper feelings, I felt out of control, unvalued, unloved, deeply unappreciated, and unaccepted, both by him and by all the board members who allowed this decision. I felt two basic emotions:

Rejection: I felt like a child who is totally rejected by a parent.

Loss: I felt like a parent whose child (ministry) is kidnapped.

Additionally, I recognized that I was in shock. With shock came the feelings of confusion and chaos.

Raw emotions like those above may or may not represent truthful thinking. Thoroughly discuss your emotions (like those in the above examples) with trusted pastors, peers, or counselors to make sure they represent reasonable conclusions. For instance, the fact that you feel unappreciated may or may not reflect a reasonable choice. Unfortunately, many Christians and ministers get discouraged and quit functioning in ministry due to feelings that they refuse to discuss, or feel uncomfortable discussing. Like their untruthful thoughts, they would probably continue working if they tried to discuss the accuracy of their feelings with some trusted individuals.

It is important for church leaders to encourage their staff and ministers to discuss their thoughts and feelings. Especially during transition, failure to seek input from others can result in negative interpretation.

Step 4—Dialog, if Possible

Problems and conflicts are inevitable on every team, Christian or not. Although normal individuals dislike conflict, dialog serves a fruitful purpose if carefully orchestrated: it helps to identify a bigger picture, it enables each party to vent pent-up emotions, it enables members to strengthen their self-image by expressing their insights and emotions, and it promotes a belief that each individual is valued. Although a conflict includes a significant destructive potential, it also includes some positive aspects—to generate jointly owned solutions and to create empathy for differing viewpoints. However, the positive aspects often remain unrealized and make the conflict unhealthy. For this reason, most of us fear conflict. And, those who do not fear conflict often inflict pain on the rest of us. Although inevitable, conflicts can produce extremely productive results. To benefit the most, enter it with well-planned strategies and well-practiced tactics.

Unfortunately, many Christians withdraw completely and avoid conflict. Perhaps they believe that a conflict represents sin. However,

Jesus, the Apostle Paul, and many other biblical figures engaged in conflict, without sinning.

Conflict with Well-Planned Strategies

The Apostle Paul placed love above all strategies and principles. Newlyweds, college students, best friends, and church staffs turn to 1 Corinthians for a clear definition of love:

> Love is patient, love is kind. It does not envy, it does not boast, it is not proud. It is not rude, it is not self-seeking, it is not easily angered, it keeps no record of wrongs. Love does not delight in evil but rejoices with the truth. It always protects, always trusts, always hopes, always perseveres (13:4-7).

When individuals fail to live up to expectations or make mistakes, love continues to communicate, even in the absence of words, even in the presence of conflict. Robert Banks explains that this attitude of love "details not so much individuals' relationship with God as the interaction between Christian brothers and sisters. These attitudes should accompany their communication with one another and should also lead them into a real depth of relationship with one another" (Banks 53). A conflict without love means that Satan wins the conflict, and you lose regardless of the outcome. A power-based move preserves self-interests, and therefore almost always neglects justice, mercy, and kindness. Since power-based moves almost always fail to show love, Satan usually wins these conflicts.

A strategy is a carefully devised plan of action to achieve a goal. As Christians, our primary goal includes showing agape love even while we intensely disagree with each other. We recommend the following behaviors and strategies for showing love even in the midst of conflict:

1. Strategy—avoid starting from a point of power or trying to win an argument through a power play—instead, follow the biblical pattern with your complaint.

Jesus instructed the aggrieved party to talk personally and privately with the individual who acted wrongly (Matthew 18:15). This approach helps to reduce power differences. If a personal (one on one) discussion fails to produce clarification and resolve the conflict, take a second step—take one or two other individuals along to help with the reconciliation process. Then after failing to resolve the matter with a couple of trusted individuals, Jesus suggested taking the matter to the entire church body. If this final step failed to bring resolution, the last resort was excommunication from the church community (Mounce, 117). Following this pattern requires courage.

However, when Christians implment a power-based approach they fail to follow the biblical model. They structure the meetings to prevent or withdraw from dialog. And when your proponent prevents dialog, Satan wins.

2. Strategy—avoid withdrawal—instead, turn toward your protagonist.

Withdrawal rarely resolves a disagreement because communication ceases while negative interpretation, blaming, and mind reading proliferate. Withdrawal also gives each party time to implement additional passive-aggressive behaviors. So, withdrawal tends to reinforce negative opinions and negative behavior. Although an out-and-out conflict inflicts pain, avoidance usually leads to much greater pain downstream. Consciously choose to avoid withdrawal if possible. Instead, intentionally search for ways to meet your protagonist face-to-face.

3. Strategy— avoid venting your negative emotions all at once— instead, express negative emotions a little at a time.

Emotions remain important and deserve expression. However, Ephesians 4:29 says, "Do not let any unwelcome talk come out of your mouths, but only what is helpful for building others up..."

4. Strategy—avoid the quick-fix approach—instead, seek discussion and understanding.

The quick fix rarely addresses the deeper issues. The unaddressed issues stimulate each individual to ruminate or dwell on their injured feelings. Avoid jumping to solutions—consciously choose to discuss all aspects of the issue without bringing up quick-fix solutions. Although you may spend more time in dialog, you will almost always spend less time in conflict.

5. Strategy—avoid surprises—instead, anticipate problems and plan to address them.

a. First, make sure that all parties feel fully committed to resolve the problem and want to continue the relationship. Otherwise, discuss the inevitable relationship failure.

b. Make sure that all stakeholders participate. If you inadvertently or purposely avoid inviting a stakeholder, expect wheel-spinning, negative interpretation, and mind reading, not to mention hurt feelings.

c. If at all possible, discuss your viewpoints and stances with several unbiased mentors prior to the discussion. Look to someone other than your superiors for this important feedback.

d. Pray for Holy Spirit guidance and insight. Especially pray that you can exhibit Christ-like attitudes during the conflict.

6. Strategy—avoid acting dogmatic—instead, show acceptance of your peer's personality by listening and allowing them to influence you.

Instead of accepting our protagonists with all of their personality quirks, we sometimes want to change them. We assume that by changing them, we win our argument. This approach merely invalidates their personality. Even if someone exhibits a personality disorder, you can still learn how to get along in spite of the disorder. The solution to any problem starts with acceptance of personality differences along with long-term commitment to work past those differences. Avoid trying to change others, and instead accept their influence.

Emotionally intelligent team members welcome the opportunity to learn from one another and accept influence from each other. They listen all the more intently when they disagree. To show acceptance of your peers, work to create an atmosphere in which they feel understood, accepted, and non-judged.

7. Strategy—don't waste time trying to solve unsolvable problems—instead, determine whether your issues are solvable or perpetual.

Most issues remain unsolvable and perpetual. Perpetual problems usually result from personality and background differences. Therefore, you accept a host of perpetual problems with every team member, including every newly hired team member. Since personality differences affect every team, you can never completely eliminate disagreements. Perpetual problems destroy teams that fail to implement appropriate skills.

8. Strategy—don't waste time arguing about non-negotiable issues—instead recognize the difference between negotiable and non-negotiable issues.

Non-negotiable issues might be:

To refrain from shouting or acting violent

To not risk another's credentials without absolute proof

To respect and honor others

To guard the integrity of others

Negotiable issues might be:

To determine who to involve in the discussion

To use active listening

To use clear and honest communication

To respect the needs of others through disarming and take-five

To identify the hidden issues

To remain open to new information and data

To persist in focusing on the problem at hand

To keep working toward a win-win (or "no loser") solution

To refuse control and power (I win-you lose) solutions or abdication (I lose-you win) solutions.

9. Strategy—Demonstrate love by your willingness to compromise on perpetual problems.

Perpetual problems remain unsolvable. However, you can almost always reach a compromise after a thorough discussion. Implement the active listening skills to ensure clarity. If you still fail to reach a compromise, four choices remain:

1. "Fence" the topic to keep the conflict from affecting other aspects of your relationship. Fencing becomes necessary

when individuals adhere to basic difference in values, or suffer from depression, Bi-polar, or other personality disorders. If you suspect that your colleague suffers from a personality disorder, insist that he or she seek a professional assessment from a psychologist or physician. Regardless, fence your differences, but only after a prolonged dialog fails to reach a compromise. Otherwise, fencing actually represents withdrawal.

2. Seek counsel to help you cope with your differences.
3. Leave relationships that result in habitual abuse.
4. As a last resort, leave the relationship. This indicates that either you remain unsuccessful in implementing the relationship skills, or the other party remains unwilling to dialog or compromise. If you conflict with a supervisor who refuses to dialog (habitually withdraws), find another job. Otherwise, you will suffer from habitual abuse and power-based behavior.

Use Conflict-Controlling Tactics

A tactic is a method that achieves an immediate or short-term goal. To conflict effectively on any team requires the following tactics:

1. Tactic—If a conflict breaks out unexpectedly, and you feel unprepared, take-five to retreat, gather information, and prepare for the conflict.

During the take-five break, consult with unbiased mentors, reflect on the issues, calm your emotions, and consider ways to implement the disarming principles. However, a long break may allow your protagonists the opportunity to engage in passive-aggressive behavior. Once a conflict erupts, opt for several short take-five sessions in lieu of a single longer session.

2. Tactic—Take responsibility for your own behavior. Romans 12:18 says, "If it is possible, as far as it depends on you, live in peace.

Recognize that not everything depends on you or your behavior, especially if someone in the disagreement suffers from a personality disorder. Thus, some problems remain perpetual regardless your desire to fix them.

3. Tactic—From start to finish, implement the rules for active listening. Limit those who would go on and on—addressing multiple issues at a time.

4. Tactic—If a conflict breaks out, avoid trying to solve the problem. At the same time do not let others begin the solution process until you take time to thoroughly discuss the issues.

Prolonged discussions often spawn new ideas. Proverbs 18:13 says, "If one gives answer before hearing it is folly and shame." Most North Americans try to jump directly to problem solution before they discuss and thoroughly define the issues. Leave problem solving for the last skill, not the first. When you hear others jumping ahead to problem solution, encourage them to further discuss the issues, exhausting every possible aspect.

5. Tactic—Help others paraphrase their complaints.

If you notice contempt, especially in body language, address it immediately by helping others state their disappointment appropriately.

Jesus consistently taught the importance of speaking truthfully and lovingly. However, He indicated, that at times disagreement would remain inevitable. In these situations, He suggested that the individuals in disagreement seek understanding and clarification regarding the conflicting issues. Matthew 18:15 presents His model for seeking clarification: "If your brother sins against you, go and show him his fault, just between the two of you. If he listens to you, you have won your brother over."

Jesus encouraged His followers to confront the disturbing and conflicting issues in their relationships. His model of addressing conflict in Matthew presents a clear example of assertive communication. It leaves no room for guessing or assigning blame to the individual who acted wrongly. Rather, this model invites dialog and sets the stage for problem solving.

6. Tactic—Search diligently for potential hidden issues—address power and control issues individually in a culturally appropriate manner.

7. Tactic—If conflict continues to escalate or progress seems slow, take a break, then agree to talk later.

Sometimes, even a five minute break helps each individual to see the issues more clearly. If you use take a break, set up a time to resume the discussion. If you need a break due to escalation, agree to start back with active listening skills.

8. Tactic—Privately correct faulty thinking or inappropriate behavior.

Correction that takes place in front of others almost always causes embarrassment.

9. Tactic—Meet in a neutral place. Make sure that your meeting place remains quiet without distractions of children, outside noise, or those who might intrude.

10. Tactic—Sit face-to-face with the protagonist so you can observe body language.

This means that you intentionally choose to avoid e-mail and internet communication during conflict. E-mail and social media promote negative interpretation and mind reading. If you must use the phone in lieu of a face-to-face meeting, find a highly trained mediator to serve as a go-between. Otherwise implement a video camera at each location (along with the phone) so that each participant can see facial expressions and body language. The video camera helps convey important cues that remain misinterpreted through a phone or internet connection. While e-mail serves a useful purpose to record and transmit information (such as the results of your conversation), it remains the worst media for dialog. Face-to-face meetings may cost several thousand dollars in airfare, but the long-term cost pales in comparison to the loss of a relationship. Ask yourself, "Would I rather spend a couple thousand dollars to resolve this issue face-to-face, or spend the rest of my life trying to recover from the loss of this relationship and the result of conflict?" Because the schedules for any two ministers rarely coincide with each other, they often try to resolve conflict through e-mail. If you care about the result of the conflict, don't accept e-mail limitations. Honor your relationship with the best two-way dialog possible.

11. Tactic—Limit the sessions to two hours maximum, and plan to finish by 8:00 p.m.

Any session longer than two hours tends to generate inattention. When people tire, they tend to interpret words negatively. Allow time for all participants to fully engage, and when they show signs of weariness, hunger, or inattention, schedule a follow-up discussion. Rather than risk escalation and flared tempers, take a break. Because people will continue to think about an intense discussion for the next two to three hours, meetings that last late into the evening almost always turn negative and promote sleeplessness.

Step 5—Reframe the events

Consider the following questions and how they relate specifically to your incident:

1. Why would God allow this bad thing (the abuse) to happen to a good person? Answer— bad things are as likely to happen to Christians as anyone else.

2. Why do I feel out of control? Answer— many things remain beyond our control. And, God allows us to control much of our lives even when we cannot control everything.

3. Why is the world so unsafe? Answer— the world is a tough place but people will usually help those who request help. Regardless, God abides with us during times of need.

4. Is this crisis a punishment or part of my destiny? Answer— sometimes bad events happen, not according to any particular plan, but just by chance. Avoid designating the crisis as a punishment or destiny. Any such designation puts you into the role of God, and sets you up as a judge. Only God knows His intentions. Avoid acting as a judge of His intentions.

5. Why does life feel so meaningless? Answer— you can find meaning in relationships with other people and with God.

Note that each of the above questions starts with, "Why." Try to reframe your "Why" questions into a "How" or "What" questions.

Application:

Continuing with the same incident described in the above steps, pastor John felt abused and wanted to resign from ministry. However, instead of focusing on the incident, he gradually forced himself to refocus on his unmistakable call to serve. He reframed his feeling of meaninglessness by noting that he could still serve in numerous ways. He felt meaningfulness prior to that ministry assignment, and he knew that God would help him find a meaningful place to serve in spite of the incident.

First, he found others with whom to discuss his thoughts and feelings. Then, he considered the questions above, and reports that he found the following truths as he refocused his service and considered each of the above reframing questions:

1. God allows injustice even though He still promotes justice and kindness. He allows bad things to happen to me and other Christians. In their pursuit of power and control, humans sometimes neglect justice and mercy. And sometimes they simply make a mistake.

2. I felt out of control as others took over my responsibilities. I concluded that I cannot control everything in my work environment, but I can control how I recover.

3. The work environment felt very unsafe and uncaring. In spite of an apparent lack of care by the senior pastor, some individuals expressed great care and concern in the middle of the incident. I reflected on the trials and abuses faced by the Apostle Paul. I concluded that even when I feel unsafe, God cares and so do some of His followers.

4. God was not punishing me. This incident merely offered an unsolicited opportunity for personal and spiritual growth.

5. Life initially felt meaningless as I went through a transition of refocusing my efforts toward a different ministry in another church. In the end, I found meaning in deeper relationships with God and friends, not from any particular ministry and not even from the act of serving others.

6. Along with a difficult transition, God eventually steered me

toward a more challenging ministry with even more ministry responsibilities. Though more difficult, the new opportunity also offers more meaningfulness than my previous ministry.

7. My heightened desire to pursue God offers a greater redemption from the incident than my desire to find meaningfulness in ministry.

8. I expected that my senior pastor and board members would engage in an open and prolonged dialog. What seemed like power-based actions (decisions without my input or consent) collided with my expectations for justice and mercy (kindness). Thus, my inflated expectations of others also fed my disappointment. I adjusted by expectations to more accurately reflect that Christians remain human.

9. I kept reminding myself that power-based exploitation (see definition on page 2) always remains inappropriate. God says, "But you have neglected the more important matters of the law—justice, mercy, and faithfulness." So when I now witness a lack of justice or mercy (kindness), I know that the problem originates in humankind's desires, not God's. He values justice and kindness.

10. I keep reminding myself that I have inadvertently hurt other Christians, too. I also retain imperfections. I need forgiveness, too, and will probably need it many times again.

Lastly, by refocusing on thankfulness (see next chapter), pastor John is gradually overcoming a fear of his church organization. This fear prompts him to avoid connecting deeply with ministers from his own organization. His lifetime experiences keep saying, "They will hurt you again, just like they did in the past. Stay away from them. Ministers are dangerous." He tells himself, cognitively, that these statements remain untrue. He chooses to constantly remind himself of the many ministers who have mentored him with kindness and justice.

Reflection:

Identify past hurts that you have avoided addressing directly.

Describe how that avoidance affects your past choices and your present situation.

Address a past hurt using the five-step model above.

How do you now feel about the incident after implementing the model?

CHAPTER 5

Using Thankfulness
To Overcome Hurt

Someone asked me to define the opposite of thankfulness. Many individuals consider envy and covetousness as opposites to thankfulness. In some ways they are right. Psychologically, however, fear and thankfulness operate in a mutually exclusive manner. That is, recent research shows that the brain cannot physically process fear while simultaneously processing thankfulness. Thus, research and the Bible agree, "There is no fear in love. But perfect love drives out fear, because fear has to do with punishment. The one who fears is not made perfect in love" (1 John 4:18, NIV). Love produces thankfulness, which in turn excludes fear. So thankfulness operates as an antidote to fear. Christians sometimes hurt each other. Hurt breeds fear. But as they develop thankfulness, they experience less fear.

Anxiety disorders routinely disable many Christians. Effective medications calm those with an anxiety disorder; however, thankfulness also calms anxiety. The spiritual exercise of counting one's blessings provides as much of an emotional lift as a spiritual lift.

Thankfulness: why is it important?

Emmons and McCullough (2003) looked at gratitude and thanksgiving in everyday life. For ten weeks, subjects were asked to complete a weekly log of their emotions, physical symptoms, and health behaviors. One-third of them were asked to simply record up to five major events or circumstances that most affected them during the week. One-third of the subjects were asked to write five hassles or minor stressors that occurred in their life in the past week. The final third were asked to write five things in their lives for which they were grateful. Additionally, they evaluated their life as a whole during the past week and their expectation for the upcoming week.

At the conclusion of ten weeks, the three groups showed significant differences. Relative to the hassles and events group, participants in the gratitude group felt better about their lives as a whole and were more optimistic about their expectations for the upcoming week. Over all, the thankful group reported fewer physical complaints than the hassles group and spent significantly more time exercising than the subjects in the other two groups. Please access the YouTube playlist available at:

http://www.youtube.com/playlist?list=PL72D988EF1CB77905

to view the video titled "Robert Emmons: The Power of Gratitude."

Additionally, Emmons found that a daily gratitude intervention (self-guided exercise) resulted in higher reported levels of the positive states of alertness, enthusiasm, determination, attentiveness, and energy compared to a focus on hassles or a downward social comparison (ways in which participants thought they were better off than others). There was no difference in levels of unpleasant emotions reported in the three groups.

Participants in the daily gratitude condition were more likely to report having helped someone with a personal problem or having offered emotional support to another, relative to the hassles or social comparison condition.

The gratitude intervention seemed to cause an interesting side effect. At the beginning of the study, individuals were asked to write down six goals or projects they intended to pursue over the next two months. Two months later, they evaluated the degree of progress they had made on each of these six pursuits. Specifically, they were asked to rate how successful they had pursued their goals, noting how much progress they had made toward each goal and how satisfied they felt with their amount of progress. On average, participants who had been in the gratitude group reported making more progress toward their goals than participants in the other two groups. This fascinating finding suggests that the benefits of an attitude of gratitude extend beyond the domain of mood and well-being to encompass more specific indicators of successful living—the attainment of concrete goals in life. The study provides empirical confirmation of the saying that "thanksgiving leads to having more to give thanks for," and that there are benefits to "counting one's blessings, one by one" (Templeton, 1997).

In a follow-on study of adults with neuromuscular disease, a 21-day gratitude intervention resulted in greater amounts of high energy, positive moods, a greater sense of feeling connected to others, more optimistic ratings of one's life, and better sleep duration and sleep quality—relative to a control group.

Other important benefits of gratefulness include:

Well-Being: Grateful people report higher levels of positive emotions, life satisfaction, vitality, optimism, and lower levels of depression and stress. The disposition toward gratitude appears to enhance pleasant feeling states more than it diminishes unpleasant emotions. Grateful people do not deny or ignore the negative aspects of life.

Pro-sociality: People with a strong disposition toward gratitude have the capacity to be empathic and to take the perspective of others. They are rated as more generous and more helpful by people in their social networks (McCullough, Emmons, & Tsang, 2002).

Spirituality: Those who regularly attend religious services and engage in religious activities such as prayer (and reading religious material) are more likely to feel grateful. Grateful people are more likely to acknowledge a belief in the interconnectedness of all life and a commitment and responsibility to others (McCullough et. al., 2002).

Materialism: Grateful individuals place less importance on material goods. They are less likely to judge their own and others' success in terms of possessions accumulated, less envious of wealthy persons, and more likely to share their possessions, compared to less grateful persons.

Gratefulness: not the same as indebtedness

Christians sometimes feel indebtedness to other Christians, and even to God. In studying the difference between gratefulness and indebtedness, Gray & Emmons (2000) found that people who write about being indebted to others report higher levels of anger and lower levels of appreciation, happiness, and love—relative to people who write about being grateful. Additionally, the experience of indebtedness is less likely to lead to a desire to approach or make contact with others—relative to an experience of gratefulness. Thus, indebtedness tends to be an aversive psychological state that is quite different from gratitude. What are some ways that your feelings of indebtedness possibly stimulate a lower level of appreciation rather than feelings of gratitude?

Thankfulness: how to develop it

Mitchel Adler (2001) defines eight aspects of appreciation. To develop thankfulness, try the following eight-week program. By the end, you will discover deep feelings of thankfulness, be more appreciative of others, and sing praises to God.

Exercise: A positive statement, or thought, followed by a task is given for each day. Think about each statement and repeat it to yourself many times throughout the day. In some cases the thought may not seem to apply to your situation, especially if your thankfulness has degraded to feelings of indebtedness. Keep in mind that the statement does not have to describe you at the present time. If you can think of a single instance or episode where the statement applies, focus on that memory. Also try to complete the simple task that follows each positive statement. Make sure to complete the task for each day, no matter how you happen to feel that day. Do not stop even if unpleasant things have occurred.

Although this exercise might sound silly, it comes from a wide body of research. This approach is one of the tenets of cognitive therapy, which has proven highly successful. If, over time, you deliberately accustom your mind to thinking on the good things in life, your outlook will change. What Scriptures support this principle?

Week 1: Have focus—What do you *have* for which you feel appreciative? (Note that what you have is not only confined to material possessions but also includes possessions that are not tangible.)

Monday:

> Thought: I am genuinely blessed by tangible things that God and others have provided.
>
> Task: List your physical blessings in this world.

Tuesday:

> Thought: I am blessed with opportunities.
>
> Task: List the opportunities God has provided and write a paragraph about them.

Wednesday:

> Thought: I am fortunate.
>
> Task: Choose two things for which you are particularly fortunate and write a few sentences about them.

Thursday:

> Thought: I am blessed with good things in life.
>
> Task: List some good things that God provides from which you receive pleasure.

Friday:

> Thought: I appreciated many specific qualities in my coworkers.
>
> Task: Write down one characteristic for each coworker that you appreciate.

Describe your insights after **Week 1** of this exercise.

Week 2: Awe—What makes you sometimes stand in *awe*?

Monday:

> Thought: I feel a genuine sense of awe at how God has guided my life and ministry.

Task: List the ways that God has guided your life and ministry.

Tuesday:

Thought: I am fortunate to be alive.

Task: List specific past events where God intervened to protect you and your family.

Wednesday:

Thought: I am in awe of how God has designed nature.

Task: List at least two things in nature that provide you with an emotional connection to God.

Thursday:

Thought: I am blessed with miracles that God still is performing in my life and in the lives of those I love.

Task: List some ways that God is still in the process of performing a miracle in your life and in the lives of your loved ones.

Friday:

Thought: I admire or appreciate my coworkers.

Task: How is the hand of God evident in His selection of the role of your coworkers in your life?

Describe your insights after **Week 2** of this exercise.

Week 3: *Rituals*—What specific acts or *rituals* do you use to give thanks to the Lord and to others?

Monday:

Thought: God guides my life and ministry through the rituals that He has put in my live.

Task: List the specific rituals or events that remind you to give thanks on a regular basis.

Tuesday:

Thought: I want to purposefully give thanks to God.

Task: List some ways that you can remind yourself purposefully to give thanks to God.

Wednesday:

Thought: I want to purposefully give thanks to those I love.

Task: List some ways that you can remind yourself purposefully to give thanks to your loved ones.

Thursday:

Thought: I want to purposefully give thanks to those with whom I work.

Task: List some ways that you can remind yourself purposefully to give thanks to those with whom you work.

Friday:

Thought: I want to purposefully give thanks to those who dislike me or who hurt me.

Task: List some ways that you can remind yourself purposefully to give thanks to those who dislike you or hurt you.

Describe your insights after **Week 3** of this exercise.

Week 4: Present moment—In what ways do you stop to appreciate the *present moment* even while you are experiencing it?

Monday:

Thought: God provides beautiful things in nature for me to enjoy every day.

Task: List at least two aspects of nature that I see every day but sometimes fail to stop and appreciate.

Tuesday:

Thought: God gives me wonderful work and ministry to enjoy every day.

Task: List at least two positive things about your work and ministry that you sometimes fail to stop and appreciate.

Wednesday

Thought: God gives me relationships to enjoy every day.

Task: List at least two things about the people in your everyday life that you sometimes fail to stop and appreciate.

Thursday:

Thought: God orchestrates wonderful events in my everyday life.

Task: List at least two events in your everyday life that you sometimes fail to stop and appreciate.

Friday:

Thought: God gives me wonderful leaders in my everyday life.

Task: List at least two ways that you sometimes fail to stop and appreciate your leaders.

Describe your insights after **Week 4** of this exercise.

*Week 5: Social comparison*s—By remembering some individuals who are less fortunate than yourself, are you periodically reminded to take note of your blessings?

Monday:

Thought: God blesses me in comparison to the others around me.

Task: List some ways that God blesses you in comparison to others.

Tuesday:

Thought: God blesses me in comparison to my coworkers.

Task: List some ways that God blesses you in comparison to those with whom you work.

Wednesday:

Thought: God blesses me in comparison to my leaders.

Task: List some ways that God blesses you in comparison to your leaders.

Thursday:

Thought: God blesses me in comparison to my relatives.

Task: List some ways that God blesses you in comparison to your relatives.

Friday:

Thought: God blesses me in comparison to others.

Task: List some ways that God blesses you in comparison to other ministers.

Describe your insights after **Week 5** of this exercise.

Week 6: Gratitude—In what ways are you grateful?

Monday:

Thought: God blesses me through the sacrifices of others.

Task: List the sacrifices that others have made on your behalf for which you are presently grateful.

Tuesday:

Thought: Others bless me in ways that I can never repay.

Task: List the emotional or monetary debts to others that you can never repay.

Wednesday:

Thought: God blesses me with opportunities.

Task: What are some of the opportunities you have experienced for which you feel grateful?

Thursday:

Thought: God blesses me uniquely.

Task: For what are you especially thankful to God (what has He done uniquely for you)?

Friday:

    Thought: God blesses me with love that I never earned.

    Task: List some ways that you receive love that you never earned.

Describe your insights after **Week 6** of this exercise.

Week 7: Loss and adversity—What personal *losses and adversities* have reminded you of how fortunate you really are?

Monday:

    Thought: God blesses me with personal problems.

    Task: What personal problems remind you to value the positive aspects of life?

Tuesday:

    Thought: God blesses me with challenges.

    Task: What personal challenges remind you to value the positive aspects of life?

Wednesday:

    Thought: God blesses me with losses.

    Task: What losses remind you to value life?

Thursday:

    Thought: God blesses me with relationship conflict.

    Task: What relationship struggles remind you to value others?

Friday:

    Thought: God blesses me with adversity.

    Task: What, in particular, reminds you to live every day to the fullest?

Describe your insights after **Week 7** of this exercise.

Week 8: Interpersonal relationships—For what interpersonal relationships are you appreciative?

Monday:

    Thought: God blesses me with people who care and show commitment to my well-being.

    Task: List the people who care about you.

Tuesday:

    Thought: God blesses me with people who understand me.

    Task: List the people who understand you.

Wednesday:

    Thought: God blesses me with people who I like to be around.

    Task: List the people who you like to be around.

Thursday:

    Thought: God blesses me with people who mentor me.

    Task: List the people who mentor you, sometimes even unknowingly.

Friday:

    Thought: God blesses me with people who help me.

    Task: List the people who serve interdependently with you.

Describe your insights after **Week 8** of this exercise.

CHAPTER 6

Words That Heal in a World That Hurts

In 1943, fourteen year old Jim Davis (my father) caught tuberculosis, an almost certain death sentence at that time. No antibiotics yet existed for the terrible disease. He remembers hearing the local doctor tell his mother that her son would almost certainly die. In a tuberculosis hospital, however, a visiting minister introduced him to the Bible. Following his conversion, my dad experienced instantaneous spiritual and physical healing. Sixty-one years later, he retired after serving 48 years as a foreign missionary. Today, Dad notes that, other than his decision to become a Christian, the suffering of tuberculosis brought the most positive results to his life. God helped him reframe suffering into hope. And hope produced a lifetime of service.

A Theological Perspective

Why does God allow Christians to suffer? Is God punishing me when He allows a death or a crisis to happen? Where was God during my crisis? If I had more faith could I have avoided this disaster? For Christians, these questions seem tough to answer. Yet, throughout the Old and New Testament we discover evidence that believers suffered in a world that seems desperately unfair.

This chapter defines a biblical theology of suffering and gives guidelines on how to help Christians who experience pain. Almost all individuals experiences one or more crisis during their lifetime. A crisis often causes an individual to question his or her faith. Research indicates that within two years after a crisis, 25% of people will turn agnostic due to their crisis. Another 25% will transition to a different faith. For Christians, helping others recover in times of crisis provides an opportunity to:

1. Share their faith with people who previously resisted the gospel.
2. Strengthen the faith of believers who might otherwise struggle.

Although the Bible contains numerous accounts of suffering, some evangelicals view Christianity as a guarantee for a pain-free world. These folks seem to continually look for an opportunity for a fulfilled, meaningful life NOW. The teaching of the prosperity gospel includes a myth that Christians will have a good time on this earth with protection from poverty and pain. C.S. Lewis addresses this issue in answer to the question, "why a Christian should not expect an easy life."

Because God is forcing him on, or up, to a higher level: putting him into situations where he will have to be very much braver, or more patient, or more loving, than he ever dreamed of being before. It seems to us all unnecessary, but that is because we have not yet had the slightest notion of the tremendous thing He means to make of us." (Mere Christianity).

A "normal" Christian therefore may expect to experience crisis and trouble as part of a normal earthly experience. And the crisis journey, when properly focused, results in growth. With time, the walk through pain will lead to a deeper desire to know God, resulting in indescribable joy. No biblical basis supports a theology for the absence of suffering. However, we have the assurance that God will faithfully walk with us, AND take us past suffering to even a better place than where we have been.

The Old Testament book of Ruth offers an excellent example of suffering. Naomi, Ruth's mother-in-law, depicts a godly woman in emotional pain. A widow who buried two sons, Naomi possessed every reason to grieve. As we read through the story, we discover that her pain resulted in a higher purpose. Her daughter-in-law remarries and presents Naomi with a grandson. Decades later, Naomi's grandson becomes the grandfather of King David, and part of the earthly family through whom Jesus entered the world. Naomi never saw all of the higher purpose. But she rejoiced in her grandson.

Another biblical account describes the unjust treatment of Joseph in prison. Although he lived a sanctified life before prison, he reached even deeper depths of spirituality through suffering. "But while Joseph was there in the prison, the Lord was with him" (Gen. 39:20-21). God did not immediately change the circumstances; He was, however, with Joseph through the circumstances.

We cannot ignore the story of Job. From beginning to end, Job endured every form of physical, emotional, and spiritual suffering. Although Job questioned, he received few answers. He discovered that in losing all of his material possessions he gained a very close relationship with God. At one point he courageously stated, "Though he slay me, yet will I hope in him" (Job 13:15).

In the New Testament, Jesus promised His followers that they world would not always be a safe place. "In this world you will have trouble" (John 16:33). Even Jesus asked for deliverance from the cup of suffering when He prayed, "Father, if you are willing, take this cup from me; yet not my will, but yours be done" (Luke 22: 42). His suffering led to the gift of eternal life.

The Apostle Paul also suffered through beatings, ship wrecks, and finally martyrdom. His encouragement to the church at Corinth continues to teach believers about the importance of facing difficult times: "Therefore we do not lose heart. Though outwardly we are wasting away, yet inwardly we are being renewed day by day. For our light and momentary troubles are achieving for us an eternal glory that far outweighs them all" (2 Cor. 4:17-18).

James told believers to "Consider it pure joy, my brothers, whenever you face trials of many kinds, because you know that the testing of your faith develops perseverance. Perseverance must finish its work so that you may be mature and complete, not lacking anything" (James 1:2-4). And Peter explained, "In this you greatly rejoice though now for a little while you may have suffered grief in all kinds of trials. These have come so that your faith—of greater worth than gold, which perishes though refined by fire—may be proved genuine and may result in praise, glory and honor when Jesus Christ is revealed" (1 Peter 1:6-7).

In the end, all but one Apostle faced martyrdom, and the one who escaped martyrdom suffered as an exile on an island. The personal life of the prophets and the Apostles fails to support a gospel of prosperity with protection from poverty and pain.

Belief in divine healing does not conflict with a theology of suffering. Because Jesus suffered, died, and rose again we ALWAYS have access to spiritual healing. Jesus never, however, provided physical healing to everyone. God invites us to place our complete trust and faith in Him. Sometimes God intervenes and physically heals individuals just as He did on the pages of the New Testament. At other times, He invites you and me to walk with people who suffer, offering them spiritual, emotional, and physical support on their journey.

An Emotional Perspective

In her book, *On Death and Dying*, Elisabeth Kubler-Ross, describes five stages of accepting death. These stages describe a process meant to help *patients* who know they are actively dying. A slightly different process of six stages helps Christians who suffer abuse at the hands of other Christians. Note that these stages sometimes occur in a random order. Every person's recovery progresses differently. Time periods vary from person to person.

Shock and Numbness: When abuse takes place, many individuals experience an initial feeling of shock and numbness. Statements such as, "this cannot be happening" define the earliest hours of abuse. And for a time, it may be necessary to just sit quietly, allowing the individual to absorb the news and feel the crisis.

Chaos and Confusion: Chaos and confusion describes another stage. Helpful friends can assist in some very practical ways during this stage, offering prayer, presence, and understanding.

Resentment and Anger: At some point, victims may experience resentment and anger. They may feel deserted by other Christians and peers, left to deal with recovery on their own. Sometimes the survivors feel angry with themselves for not prevent the abuse.

Denial and Withdrawal: Another normal stage includes the desire to either deny feelings or to simply pull back and cease interacting with others. Although these represent normal feelings, if they persist too long, they can grow problematic. How long is too long? No exact answer exists because, again, everyone responds differently. However, if you notice signs of prolonged depression (different from situational depression) refer your friend or loved one to a doctor. Almost everyone needs to pull away (withdraw) for a time. This cocoon effect can seem healing. But if an individual fails to take care of their physical, emotional, spiritual needs, they need a counselor.

Acknowledgment and Pain: Eventually everyone reaches this stage, where they understand fairly well what happened. They may continue to experience pain, but they can articulate and describe their feelings. Tears may flow, but they can communicate and feel ready to share their story with others.

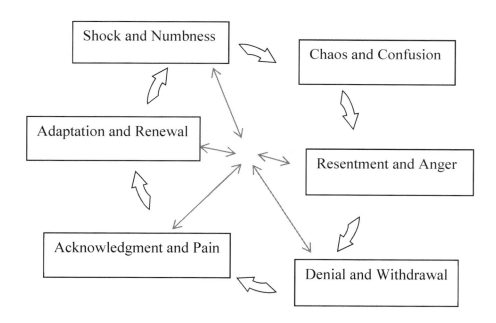

Adaptation and Renewal: This stage begins when individuals recognize that they can continue ministering and growing stronger because of their abuse. They begin to try new things, and may even begin to make meaning out of what happened. Some individuals find ways to use their abuse to help others with a similar loss.

Since these stages come and go in no particular order, think of the stages as a circular model rather than stair steps. Very early, an individual may enter the stage of adaptation and renewal, and then suddenly move back to the withdrawal stage. Or a victim might honestly acknowledge the pain one day but deny feeling pain the next. These are normal reactions during recovery.

Ministry Perspective

The word *care* finds its roots in the Gothic word *kara*, which means *lament*. The basic meaning of care is to experience sorrow, or to cry out with; care means to be present with each other. The concept of caring includes both time and space. We cannot predict a time period for recovery. In the same way, we do not need to fill space with unnecessary words. Sometimes the best gift is a gift of silence. Although everyone is capable of helping others, not everyone takes time to learn the necessary skills. Consider the following guidelines as a starting place to help others recover.

1. Avoid clichés or "God-talk" such as scriptural quotes. The victim needs compassion and emotional support, first. Common clichés to avoid include:

    Your loss must have been God's will. You shouldn't question it.

    Just trust God and you will get through this.

    God will give you another ministry to replace what you lost.

    This is an opportunity to spend more time in prayer.

God understands your sorrow.

Before making any of the above statements, ask, "How can this statement change anyone's level of pain?" Although sometimes truthful, statements such as these usually fail to help during times of deep, emotional pain.

2. Develop a "non-anxious presence" in which you simply sit in silence with the person. My wife, Beth, learned about "non-anxious presence" while working as a hospital chaplain. One evening, she sat with a woman as the doctor explained that her husband had died of a heart attack. At one point she remembers asking if she could do anything for her. The lady quickly responded, "You could stop patting my back." My wife found that she allowed her emotions (body movement) to get in the way of ministry. In fact, during traumatic events, it may be best to say nothing, simply offering your support and quiet prayers. This term that counselors refer to as "non-anxious presence" identifies the act of sitting quietly next to people in pain. Staying silent allows grieving individuals to set the agenda. If they choose to talk they will. They may prefer, however, to say nothing or to cry. They may ask for prayer. Most importantly, avoid fidgeting, and remain peaceful. Your soothing presence will serve as a calming catalyst for others around you.

3. After the initial shock of a painful event, gently engage in dialogue. When working with people in grief, allow them to tell their story. As they feel able to share, healing begins to take place. Learn to listen without sharing your own story. Use active listening skills by asking for clarification and restating what you hear. Dr. Harold Kuschner explains that

"incarnation includes God coming through people who sit with us in our pain."

4. Practice using "open" questions rather than questions that have a simple answer.

   Tell me about _____.

   I'd like to know more about your family.

   If you feel like talking, I am wondering about _____.

   What was your week like?

   What would be most helpful to you right now?

5. Sometimes, rather than speaking with clichés, simply state the obvious. When you observe what is going on, it normalizes the situation. Some examples:

   You seem overwhelmed. Is this a good time to talk?

   It sounds like you and _____ were very close.

   Those are painful feelings you're describing.

   It sounds like you might have some (regrets, anger, guilt).

6. Along with times of solitude, a lot of people find comfort in nature and music.

7. Avoid false statements (Deits, 2009) such as:

   You can never recover from a major loss such as .... (Truth— You can recover a full life after a major loss of any kind).

   Time is the only healer. (Truth—It takes time to heal, and it also takes lots of hard work).

   Nobody else can help you. (Truth—Many people can help you work through your loss, especially others who experienced similar losses.

   The death of a spouse is more painful than your loss. (Truth—any loss is painful).

   Your loss was God's will...you shouldn't question it.

(Truth—Some losses occur as a result of living in a fallen world, not by God's will). Avoid blaming or crediting the loss to anyone, especially to God.

If you just keep busy, your grief will go away. (Truth—If you keep too busy to face your feelings and avoid talking about them, you subject yourself to a higher risk of illness following a major loss).

A Personal and Spiritual Perspective

The process of recovery requires a lot of hard work. Keeping a balanced perspective is important. It is not what happens TO us that matters as much as what happen IN us.

As you recover, eventually you will feel prepared to "reframe" your situation. Proceed to address the questions below only when you have already started to consider the issues surrounding each question:

1. Why would a good God allow this bad thing (the abuse) happen to a good person? Answer— bad things are as likely to happen to Christians as anyone else.

2. Why do I feel out of control? Answer— many things remain beyond your control. And, God allows us to control much of our lives even when we cannot control everything.

3. Why is the world so unsafe? Answer— the world remains a tough place but people will usually help those who request help. Regardless, God remains present with us during our need.

4. Is this crisis a punishment or part of my destiny? Answer— sometimes bad events happen, not according to any particular plan, but just by chance. Avoid designating the crisis as a punishment or destiny. Any such designation puts you into

the role of God, and sets you up as a judge. Only God knows His intentions. Avoid acting as a judge.

5. Why does life feel so meaningless? Answer— you can find meaning in relationships with other people and with God.

Note that each of the above questions starts with, "Why." Reframe each "Why" question into a "How" or "What" question. For instance, instead of asking, "Why did God allow this to happen," reframe the question into, "How can I work through this loss?"

Note that Job asked several questions that started with "Why?" However, God never answered Job's questions. Likewise, you may never find an answer to a question that starts with "Why?" However, you can almost always find productive answers to questions that start with "How" or "What." Turning a "why" question into a "how" or "what" question usually initiates a process of personal and spiritual growth.

Beware of unhealthy addictions. In times of abuse and loss, many individuals will seek comfort through food, caffeine, drugs, or alcohol. Support groups can be very helpful for both encouragement and accountability during this time.

Also act intentionally about building relationships. Many individuals feel tempted to pull away from relationships during recovery. But they need relationships during each stage of recovery.

Discuss true statements about loss such as:

God never promised to keep us from suffering.

God can be trusted to walk with us through our suffering, and to take us past our suffering to even a better place than where we have been.

CHAPTER 7

Disciplines that Eliminate Power-Based Tendencies

Power-based exploitation cannot survive in the Christian who develops compassion, sympathy, and love. So the existence of power-based exploitation proves the lack of spiritual maturity, both in the individual and in the organization that ignores it. The *Agreeableness* personality factor represents the Biblical values of sympathy, compassion, and love. As a personality factor, *Agreeableness* is comprised of a combined assessment (an average) of five facets (Christal, 1994):

1. Warm and sympathetic
2. Friendly
3. Considerate
4. Helpful
5. Cold and insensitive (the inverse)

Scripture invites us to adopt specific lifestyles to enhance these traits. The spiritual lifestyles that build *Agreeableness* include:

1. Intercessory prayer
2. Mutual submission
3. Service and hospitality
4. Generosity

Intercessory Prayer

Jesus modeled intercessory prayer. He invites us to take our concerns to Him. As we intercede for others, we generate compassion. Even when we cannot offer money (similar to the Apostles Peter and John in Acts 3: 8-9), we can intercede and offer something more important.

Mutual Submission

Mutual submission acts as a near synonym with the *Agreeableness* facet called *Considerate*. That is, as we consider the needs of others, we mutually submit to one another.

Items in the FFM *Agreeableness* factor that relate to a lifestyle characterized by mutual submission include:

Even if I don't like them, I try always to be considerate of others.
I try to always be polite, even to those who are not polite to me.
I always treat other people with kindness.
I am always considerate of the feelings of others.
I try to be kind to everyone I know.

Because individuals high in *Agreeableness* fear rejection, they sometimes seem gullible, easily abused, and easily subjugated. Secular society often ridicules these individuals, considering their personality weak-willed and spineless. In contrast, Matt. 5: 39-41 says:

But I tell you, do not resist an evil person. If someone strikes you on the right cheek, turn to him the other also. And if someone wants to sue you and take your tunic, let him have your cloak as well. If someone forces you to go one mile, go with him two miles.

Quite possibly, Christ places a higher value on character than our ability to resist abuse.

Indeed, some individuals abused Jesus. Even as some tried to subjugate Him, He chose submissiveness by washing the feet of His followers. The mutual submission that many cultures (especially the North American culture) reject, represents the very characteristic to which Jesus calls us.

When individuals high in *Agreeableness* are also high in *Neuroticism*, co-dependency often drives a dependent personality disorder. Although therapists report that only 5 percent of their patients exhibit this disorder, up to 20 percent of the American public may suffer from a dependent personality disorder. Some cultures exhibit a rate even higher than reported in the USA.

A leader with a dependent personality disorder has the potential to devastate a congregation. The Diagnostics and Statistical Manual of Mental disorders (IV) describes this disorder as, "A pervasive and excessive need to be taken care of that leads to submissive and clinging behavior and fears of separation, beginning by early adulthood and present in a variety of contexts." The dependent personality disorder probably fuels what was referred to a few years ago as the "shepherding" movement. The leaders tended to dwell on the need for others to submit to their authority without acknowledging the Apostle Paul's balanced teaching on mutual submission. Thus, the followers grew increasingly dependent while their autocratic leader grew increasingly more autocratic, each co-dependent on the other for their dysfunctional behavior.

With up to 20 percent of the American public and even a larger percentage of other cultures suffering with a dependent personality disorder, some churches continue to flourish in this abuse. Thus, the doctrine of submission quite possibly represents the most abused doctrine in Christianity. This is not due to a lack of biblical guidance against a one-sided submission, but because secular society produces an overabundant supply of dependent individuals and autocratic leaders. Each feeds the other's dysfunction. In contrast to this dysfunction, mutual submission results from intimacy with God.

Although submission affects *Agreeableness*, when envy results from a desire for recognition, power, or authority, that desire (envy) blocks true submission. Envy of deeper issues—a desire for recognition, power, and authority can be more harmful than an envy of material possessions. Christians usually recognize their envy of material possessions, but many fail to recognize their envy of these deeper issues. These issues will often block their ability to submit in other areas of their lives. Adam and Eve possibly envied God's recognition, power, or authority more than they envied God, Himself.

Those in high positions of power experience as much difficulty with mutual submission as those without power. When envy of recognition and power motivates individuals, they tend to abuse others through obsessive control. While expecting other to submit, they lack mutual submission, themselves. They might know that a good leader should empower others by giving away power, but because they struggle with power and control issues, they are unable to give it away except for short periods—and even then, only with strings attached.

For instance, a pastor might ask his assistant to lead the church during his extended absence. Yet, he will remain involved in every aspect of the selection of preachers, sermons, and music during his absence. For these pastors, mutual submission becomes something others need to do toward them. Likewise, song leaders and other church members sometimes expect the pastor to submit to their preferences. Take a moment to reflect on the territorial sensitivity within your area of ministry. Wherever territorial sensitivity exists, the tendency toward envy of control and power often co-exist.

True submission results in freedom from envy, anxiety and nervousness. Jesus avoided bondage when He submitted to wash the feet of the apostles. Instead, He exercised freedom to submit. Ephesians 5:21 presents a picture of mutual submission when it says, "Submit to one another out of reverence for Christ."

Some Christians confuse submission with self-denial. For instance, Christ submitted to wash the feet of Peter, foreknowing that Peter would later fail. Yet, even while submitting to wash Peter's feet, Christ did not deny His own identity or self-worth. And, He illustrated the principle of mutual submission by connecting Peter's acceptance of foot washing with the ability to enter the kingdom of heaven. Neither individual denied his identity or worth, but each submitted to the other.

We sometimes misunderstand Christ's command in Matthew 16:14 when He said a follower must, "deny himself, take up his cross, and follow me." The Apostle Paul points out that we have two selves—one with the old nature and one with the new nature. Even while denying the old nature, our new nature takes up the cross and submits to Christ.

Christ did not lose His identity even as He submitted to the Jewish court system. He refused to defend Himself, yet He never hated Himself or showed the least bit of self-contempt. By freely choosing to submit, He acknowledged His true worth and identity.

Cultural factors that influence mutual submission

Cultural factors restrict submission through the following means, all based on the personality facet related to envy:

- Submission based on power—in these cultures, power provides a primary motivation. Submission based on power characterizes many Islamic cultures, but also seems present in every culture, worldwide. In these cultures:
  - Those in power refuse to submit to those with less power.
  - Overt displays of power provide the primary motivation.
  - Relationships merely provide a network to manipulate and control others.
  - Mutual submission disgraces the individual in power, and enables those in lower positions to gain power.
- Submission based on age—in some cultures, age (youth or old age) governs submission. Or, as in some Asian and African cultures, an elder cannot submit to someone younger without losing "face." Mutual submission disgraces the elder. In Western cultures, the opposite is often true. The education and energy of the youth seem more valued than the wisdom of the elderly. In either case, mutual submission fails to occur.
- Submission based on rebellion—some cultures value rebelliousness and confrontation. The most vocal rebel gains followers who admire his/her rebellious attitude. These cultures grow into societies of intimidation where mutual

submission causes everyone to appear weak-willed and spineless.

- Submission based on fatalism—some cultures embrace a fatalistic outlook on the future, believing that predestination governs everything. In these cultures, people submit because they feel helpless to control their inevitable future. Since predestination dictates who is in charge and who submits, mutual submission fails.

Practical behaviors for a lifestyle of mutual submission

Mutual submission results from a lifestyle of intimacy with God. Thus, a lifestyle of submission results not by seeking submission but by seeking intimacy with God. Ways to seek an intimate relationship with God include:

- Begin each day by asking God for humility.
- Identify ways in which your culture restricts submission through one or more of the above cultural factors. Evaluate the ways in which those beliefs and practices distort mutual submission both you and your church congregation. If you see distortions in your belief and practice of mutual submission, confess them to God.
- Form a support group with individuals above and below you in leadership. Openly discuss the cultural factors that might potentially distort the doctrine of submission.
- Identify any envy of recognition, power, and authority. If you recognize these motives, confess it to God and begin a discussion with your support group.
- Identify ways that you engage in self-abuse:
  - Self-hatred

- – Loss of identity
- – Self-contempt
- – Having an opinion that you are less significant than others

Service

Service acts as a near synonym for the *Agreeableness* facet called *Helpful*. That is, service results in acts of helpfulness to others. The *Agreeableness* assessment includes service related items such as:

Even if I don't like them, I try always to be considerate of others.
I try to always be polite, even to those who are not polite to me.
I always treat other people with kindness.
I am always considerate of the feelings of others.
I try to be kind to everyone I know.
I get a lot of pleasure in helping others with their problems.
I have a lot of sympathy for others who are having problems.
I like to help others when they are down on their luck.
I like to help others, even if there is nothing in it for me.
CONSIDERATE
HELPFUL

Christians sometimes confuse a lifestyle characterized by service with acts of service. Inspection of the above assessment items shows that this facet depends on a servant attitude more than the number of acts performed. In a lifestyle characterized strictly by acts of service, individuals may grudgingly perform numerous acts of service even while feeling inconsiderate of others.

Ephesians 4:12-13 calls pastors and teachers "to prepare God's people for works of service…until we all reach unity in the faith and in the knowledge of the Son of God and become mature." From this passage, it appears that one of the primary purposes of the pastor is to prepare God's people for service. Thus, it is not the number of people attending services, directing traffic, teaching classes, serving as greeters, or giving financially that determine the success of a church. Success for the pastor-teacher depends on how effectively he or she helps others prepare for service.

Occasionally, Christians assess the number of individuals serving, using the number itself as a success measure instead of looking at their preparedness for service. As they adopt this fallacy, individuals quickly move into positions of service with inadequate spiritual preparation. These individuals usually view service itself as the means for preparation. However, the Bible does not indicate that service, in itself, produces a change in character. If it did, then we would not see so many ministers and church deacons who fail morally. Likewise, no psychological studies reveal that service, by itself, changes personality. If anything, research shows the unchanging nature of personality in spite of acts of service. To expect that performing an act of religious service once or twice a week will change personality is, if anything, quite naïve.

In a rush to use new converts in acts of service, pastors sometimes push them prematurely into ministry, thereby preventing their preparation. Christ addressed this in Luke 10:38-42,

> Now as they went on their way, He entered a certain village, where a woman named Martha welcomed Him into her home. She had a sister named Mary who sat at the Lord's feet and listened to what he was saying. But Martha was distracted by her many tasks; so she came to Him and asked, "Lord, do you not care that my sister has left me to do all the work by myself? Tell her to help me." But the Lord answered her, "Martha, Martha, you are

worried and distracted by many things; there is need of only one thing. Mary has chosen the better part, which will not be taken away from her.

From the above Scripture, Martha possibly assumed that her service itself prepared her for an intimate relationship with the Master. Jesus explains that acts of service never substitute for intimacy.

Cultural factors that affect Service

The following cultural fallacies can hinder Christian service:

1. Leaders are valued above servants. This single cultural factor probably inhibits the implementation of a servant attitude in the Western culture more than most other values. As a general rule, Western cultures fail to value those who work in lower positions. Individuals aspire to become the president or prime minister, but rarely a servant.

2. Individuals provide service to avoid shame. Some Asian cultures use shame as a motivator. Individuals may provide service only when others can notice their efforts.

3. Service results as an obligation toward a higher position. In some cultures, parishioners serve a pastor based on his or her position. These same individuals usually refuse to serve those in lower positions and may even try to stop a church leader from serving others in lower positions.

4. Service results as an obligation of one's position. Thus, a president is obliged to provide security for those under him or her. Those with this attitude usually serve only those to whom they feel obliged. In this type of culture, service is rarely offered to strangers or enemies.

5. Service is provided only to those who can purchase it.

6. Service obligates those who receive it. In some cultures, gift

giving and service become an art, each member showing extreme care not to give too much or too little due to the resulting obligation.

7. Some positions are "above" performing servant tasks. So, only lower class individuals perform acts of service. Jesus directly confronted this cultural fallacy when He washed the feet of the disciples. When the disciples argued about who was the greatest, Jesus replied, "If anyone wants to be first, he must be the very last, and the servant of all" (Mark 9:35).

8. Only pastors are paid to serve. In this culture, Christians never aspire to a servant position.

9. Service is performed for recognition.

Practical behaviors for a lifestyle of service

Quite possibly, the *Agreeableness* personality factor represents the best case for Christianity. Believers provide a positive example of service when they:

1. Spend time daily, listening to God and learning (through Bible study) how to develop spiritual characteristics.

2. Listen and thoroughly understand others' opinions before expressing their own.

3. Serve others based on their needs instead of the believer's need to serve.

4. Focus on service rather than on results.

5. Avoid boasting about personal accomplishments. Instead, boast about God.

6. Serve anonymously, rejecting the need for recognition.

7. Serve all individuals, including both strangers and enemies.

Generosity

Items in the Agreeableness assessment that relate to a lifestyle characterized by generosity include:

I get a lot of pleasure in helping others with their problems.
I like to help others when they are down on their luck.
I like to help others, even if there is nothing in it for me.
I am always generous when it comes to helping others.
I always treat other people with kindness.
I try to be kind to everyone I know.
KIND
GENEROUS
CHEERFUL
SELFISH

Luke 11: 37-42 records what Jesus thinks about generosity,

When Jesus had finished speaking, a Pharisee invited him to eat with him; so he went in and reclined at the table. But the Pharisee, noticing that Jesus did not first wash before the meal, was surprised. Then the Lord said to him, 'Now then, you Pharisees clean the outside of the cup and dish, but inside you are full of greed and wickedness. You foolish people! Did not the one who made the outside make the inside also? But give what is inside the dish to the poor, and everything will be clean for you. Woe to you Pharisees, because you give God a tenth of your mint, rue and all other kinds of garden herbs, but you neglect justice and the love of God. You should have practiced the latter without leaving the former undone.

Two sections in the above Scripture relate directly to generosity. First, Jesus admonishes us to "give what is inside the dish to the poor."

That would include everything we are, including our time, talent, and money, but even more importantly, our future plans, future expectations, and future abilities.

Second, most individuals note the importance of practicing justice and loving God, but some overlook the second section, "without leaving the former undone." The "former" to which Jesus referred is giving God a tenth (a tithe). This supports Christ's commandment to love God. Some Christians condone a lack in generosity and tithes by ignoring this Scripture.

In addition to the commandment to love one another and love God, Christ commands two actions in the above passage—give to the poor, and give a tithe to God. Ironically, we sometimes fail to notice these two directives even though both look almost identical to the commandment to love God and love our neighbor.

Generosity often relates to one of the following two principles (Myers, 1992):

Adaptation/expectation-level principle–this principle states that we adapt to satisfaction relative to our prior expectations. That is, we compare present levels of satisfaction with past expectations. When situations change for the better or worse in relation to prior goals and expectations, levels of satisfaction change. For example, students who receive a higher grade than expected both feel good and praise their teacher; those who receive a lower grade than expected both feel upset and denigrate their teacher. Thus, a B- grade could mean something quite different to the student who expected an F as compared to a student who expected an A (Snyder and Clair, 1976).

Some Christians believe in a "name it, claim it" theology. These individuals believe that God will make each Christian physically healthy and wealthy based on a formula of giving tithes and offerings to the church. However, when these prior expectations inevitably conflict with the reality that every Christian experiences sickness and death, these individuals experience disappointment and often deny God. Their past unrealistic and erroneous expectations affect their present happiness, not to mention their generosity. The amount that a Christian gives may vary dependent on financial status, but when giving stops altogether, the *adaptation/expectation-level principle* often serves as the culprit.

Due to the *adaptation/expectation-level* principle Donald Campbell (1975) states that it would be impossible to develop a long-lasting paradise on earth. Even the happiness of a utopia without bills, sickness, and disagreements would last only for a while. Before long, we would adjust to a new adaptation level. With that new adaptation level, we would sometimes feel appreciative when expectations were exceeded, and sometimes feel disappointed when expectations were not met. For these Christians, their satisfaction remains relative to their recent past experience. In contrast, when Christians base their happiness on intimacy with God, their happiness persists. Past experiences of intimacy merely drive us to continue in intimacy.

Relative deprivation principle–This principle states that happiness is relative to others' attainment of happiness. For example, to an African making $500 a year, $10,000 probably seems like extreme wealth, but when living in New York City, where many earn over $100,000 a year, $10,000 seems like poverty. Therefore, how generous will the average two-thirds world Christian feel who compares himself/herself economically to a wealthier non-Christian, or to the subsidized ministry of an American Christian missionary? The relative deprivation principle characterizes many cultures. Pastors and church members sometimes syncretize their values of generosity and tithing to match their feeling of relative deprivation. In contrast, the Apostle Paul

(2 Cor. 8:2) praised the churches in Macedonia saying, "In the midst of a very severe trial, their overflowing joy and their extreme poverty welled up in rich generosity. For I testify that they gave as much as they were able, and even beyond their ability. Entirely on their own, they urgently pleaded with us for the privilege of sharing in this service to the Lord's people." Apparently, the Macedonian Christians rejected the relative deprivation principle.

Christians will lack generosity when they compare themselves to other people, rather than the generosity of God. The adaptation/expectation level principle and the relative deprivation principle cause a lot of failure and lack of generosity among Christians.

Cheerfulness also affects generosity. Salovey and Birnbaum (1989) call this the "feel-good, do-good phenomenon." He found that positive experiences such as success at work, reminiscing about enjoyable events, and experiencing unexpected positive events resulted in individuals giving money, volunteering time, and helping others. A cheerful mood seems to induce helpful and generous acts. Second Corinthians 9:7-8 says, "...for God loves a cheerful giver...you will abound in every good work." God seems to confirm that cheerfulness will overflow into every type of good work, even more than simple monetary generosity.

Cultural factors that influence generosity
- Love of materialism
- Insensitivity toward others
- Love of leisure
- Risk aversion

Practical behaviors for a lifestyle of generosity
Restrict credit card debt. To enable your freedom, restrict your

106   Abusive Power: When Christians Hurt Other Christians

credit card debt so you can help others and invest in them. Develop a realistic plan to eliminate all debt (1 Cor. 7:23).

Give to the poor. In Luke 12:33, Jesus says, "Sell your possessions and give to the poor. Provide purses for yourselves that will not wear out, a treasure in heaven that will not be exhausted, where no thief comes near and no moth destroys." Matthew 6:19-21 also affirms the biblical foundation to give to the poor: "Do not store up for yourselves treasures on earth, where moth and rust destroy, and where thieves break in and steal. But store up for yourselves treasures in heaven, where moth and rust do not destroy, and where thieves do not break in and steal. For where your treasure is, there your heart will be also." A minimum lifestyle is one in which you can live comfortably while accomplishing God's calling. Invest the remainder in ways that provide on-going help for others.

Tithe. Malachi 3:10 instructs, "'Test me in this,' says the Lord Almighty, 'and see if I will not throw open the floodgates of heaven and pour out so much blessing that you will not have room enough for it.'" If you do not yet tithe, start by giving a small amount. As you practice giving even a small amount, you will find that God enables you to plan and execute your financial position so that you can give more in the future. Second Corinthians 8:7 says, "But just as you excel in everything—in faith, in speech, in knowledge, in complete earnestness and in your love for us—see that you also excel in this grace of giving."

Trust God. First Timothy 6:17-18 says, "Command those who are rich in this present world not to be arrogant nor to put their hope in wealth, which is so uncertain, but to put their hope in God, who richly provides us with everything for our enjoyment. Command them to do good, to be rich in good deeds, and to be generous and willing to share. In this way they will lay up treasure for themselves as a firm foundation for the coming age, so that they may take hold of the life that is truly life."

Factor Reflection:

I will practice the following spiritual disciplines that are associated with *Agreeableness*:

My plan for practicing disciplines associated with *Agreeableness* is:

REFERENCES

Adler, M. (2001). Conceptualizing and Measuring Appreciation: The development of a new positive psychology construct. *Dissertation Abstracts International, Vol. 63, 08B.*

Bandura, A. (1986). *Social foundations of thought and action: A social cognitive theory.* Englewood Cliffs, NJ: Prentice-Hall.

Burns, David D. *The Feeling Good Handbook.* New York: Plume: 1999.

Christal, R. E (1994). *The Air Force Self-Description Inventory (AFSDI): Final R&D Status Report.* Air Force Research Laboratory, Brooks Air Force Base, San Antonio Texas, November, Metrica, Inc.

Davidson, J. C., & Caddell, D. P. (1994). Religion and the meaning of work. *Journal for the Scientific Study of Religion*, 33, 187-202.

Davis, N. W., & Davis, B. J. *Transforming Conflict: Relationship Skills for Ministers.* North Charleston, SC: CreateSpace, 2012.

Davis, N.W., & Davis, B. J. *Transforming Personality: Spiritual Formation and the Five-Factor Model.* North Charleston, SC: CreateSpace, 2012.

Deits, Bob. *Life after Loss: A Practical Guide to Renewing Your Life after Experiencing Major Loss*, Cambridge, MA: De Cappo Lifelong Books, 2009.

DeVito, Joseph A. *Messages: Building Interpersonal Communication Skills.* 2nd ed. New York: HarperCollins, 1993.

DeVito, Joseph A. *The Interpersonal Communication Book.* 2nd ed. New York: HarperCollins, 1992.

Emmons, R.A. *The Psychology of Ultimate Concerns.* New York: Guilford Press, 1999.

Emmons, R.A. & Hill, J. *Words of gratitude for mind, body, and soul*. Radnor, PA: Templeton Foundation Press, 2001.

Emmons, R.A. & Shelton, C.S. (2001). Gratitude and the science of positive psychology. In C.R. Snyder and S.J. Lopez (Eds.), *Handbook of positive psychology*. New York: Oxford University Press.

Emmons, R.A. (2001). Gratitude and mind-body health. *Spirituality and Medicine Connection, 5*, 1-7.

Emmons, R.A. (2003). Acts of gratitude in organizations. In K. S. Cameron, J. E. Dutton, & R. E. Quinn (Eds.), *Positive organizational scholarship* (pp. 81-93). San Francisco: Berrett-Koehler Publishers.

Emmons, R.A., & Crumpler, C.A. (2000). Gratitude as a human strength: Appraising the evidence. *Journal of Social and Clinical Psychology, 19,* 56-69.

Emmons, R.A., & McCullough, M.E. (2003). Counting blessings versus burdens: Experimental studies of gratitude and subjective well-being in daily life. *Journal of Personality and Social Psychology, 84,* 377-389.

Emmons, R.A., Cheung, C., & Tehrani, K. (1998). Assessing spirituality through personal goals: Implications for research on religion and subjective well-being. *Social Indicators Research*, 45, 391-422.

Emmons, R.A., McCullough, M.E., & Tsang, J. (2003). The assessment of gratitude. In S. Lopez & C.R. Snyder (Eds.), *Handbook of positive psychology assessment* (pp. 327-342) Washington, DC: American Psychological Association.

Foster, Richard J., *Celebration of Discipline: The Path to Spiritual Growth*. San Francisco: HarperCollins, 1998.

Green, Robert, *The 48 Laws of Power*, Penguin books, 2000.

Haidt, J. *The Happiness Hypothesis*. New York: Basic Books, 2006.

Kubler-Ross, Elisabeth. *On Death and Dying*, New York, NY: Scribner.1969.

Lewis, C. S. *Mere Christianity*. New York: Macmillan, 1960.

Hall-Flavin, D. K., *What is passive-aggressive behavior? What are some of the signs?* Mayo Clinic, http://www.mayoclinic.org/healthy-living/adult-health/expert-answers/passive-aggressive-behavior/faq-20057901, 2014.

Mirriam-Webster Dictionary, online definition at http://www.merriam-webster.com/dictionary/manipulate, 2014.

McCullough, M.E., Emmons, R.A., & Tsang, J. (2002). The grateful disposition: A conceptual and empirical topography. *Journal of Personality and Social Psychology*, 82, 112-127.

McCullough, M.E., Kirkpatrick, S., Emmons, R.A., & Larson, D. (2001). Is gratitude a moral affect? *Psychological Bulletin, 127,* 249-266.

Pennebaker, J. W., J. K. Kiecolt-Glaser, and T. Glaser. "Disclosure of Traumas and Immune Function: Health Implications of Psychotherapy." *Journal of Consulting and Clinical Psychology* 56 (1988): 239-245.

Peterson, C. *A primer in positive psychology*. Oxford University Press: New York, 2006.

Peterson, C., Park, N., & Seligman, M. E. P. (2006). Strengths of character and recovery. *Journal of Positive Psychology* 1.

Rowell, Jeren L. (2010). Ministerial Attrition: When Clergy Call It Quits: The Relationship of Superintendents and Pastors, ANSR Conference, March 25, 2010.

Savage, John S. *The Apathetic and Bored Church Member: Psychological and Theological Implications*. Pittsford, New York: LEED Consultants, 1976.

Seigman, M. E. P. (2002). *Authentic Happiness*. New York: Free Press.

Simon, George. *In Sheep's Clothing: Understanding and Dealing with Manipulative People*, Marion, MI: Parkhurst Brothers, (2010).

Snyder C. R., & Lopez S. J. *The Handbook of Positive Psychology*, New York: Oxford University Press, 2002.

Snyder, C. R. *Handbook of Hope: Theory, Measures, & Applications*. San Diego, CA: Academic Press, 2000.

.

ABOUT THE AUTHOR

 Nathan Davis grew up in Japan, the son of missionaries Dr. Jim and Genevieve Davis. Before becoming a minister with the Assemblies of God, he served the U.S. Air Force as a psychologist for 29 years.

Presently, Nathan serves as a foreign missionary with HealthCare Ministries. He challenges pastors on the importance of self-care issues such as relationship enhancement, crisis debriefing, spiritual formation, resilience, and retirement. He and his wife, Beth, have co-authored seven books and developed a website on self-care issues for ministers across all denominations (see www.pastorselfcare.com).

Made in the USA
Charleston, SC
21 May 2014